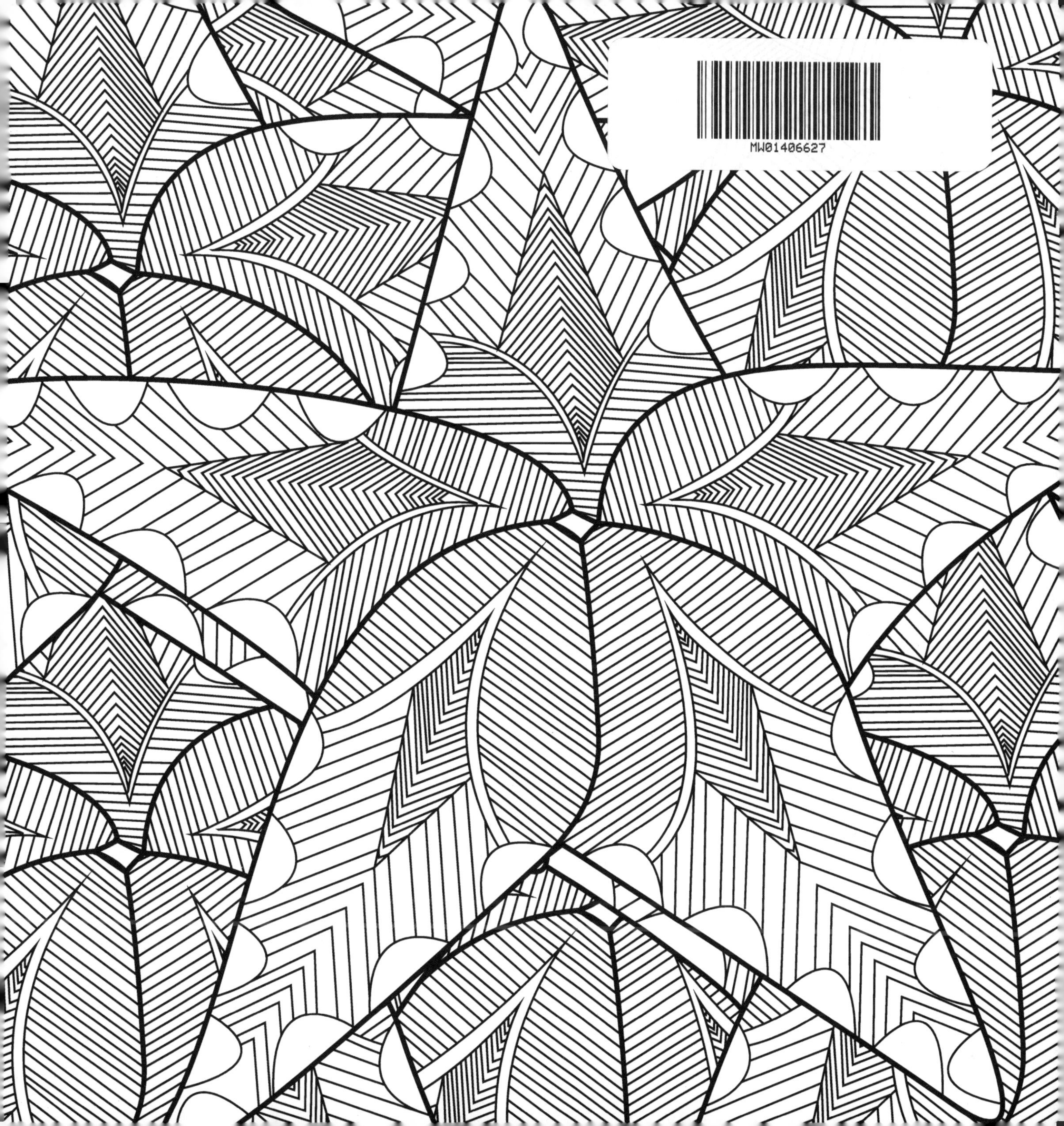

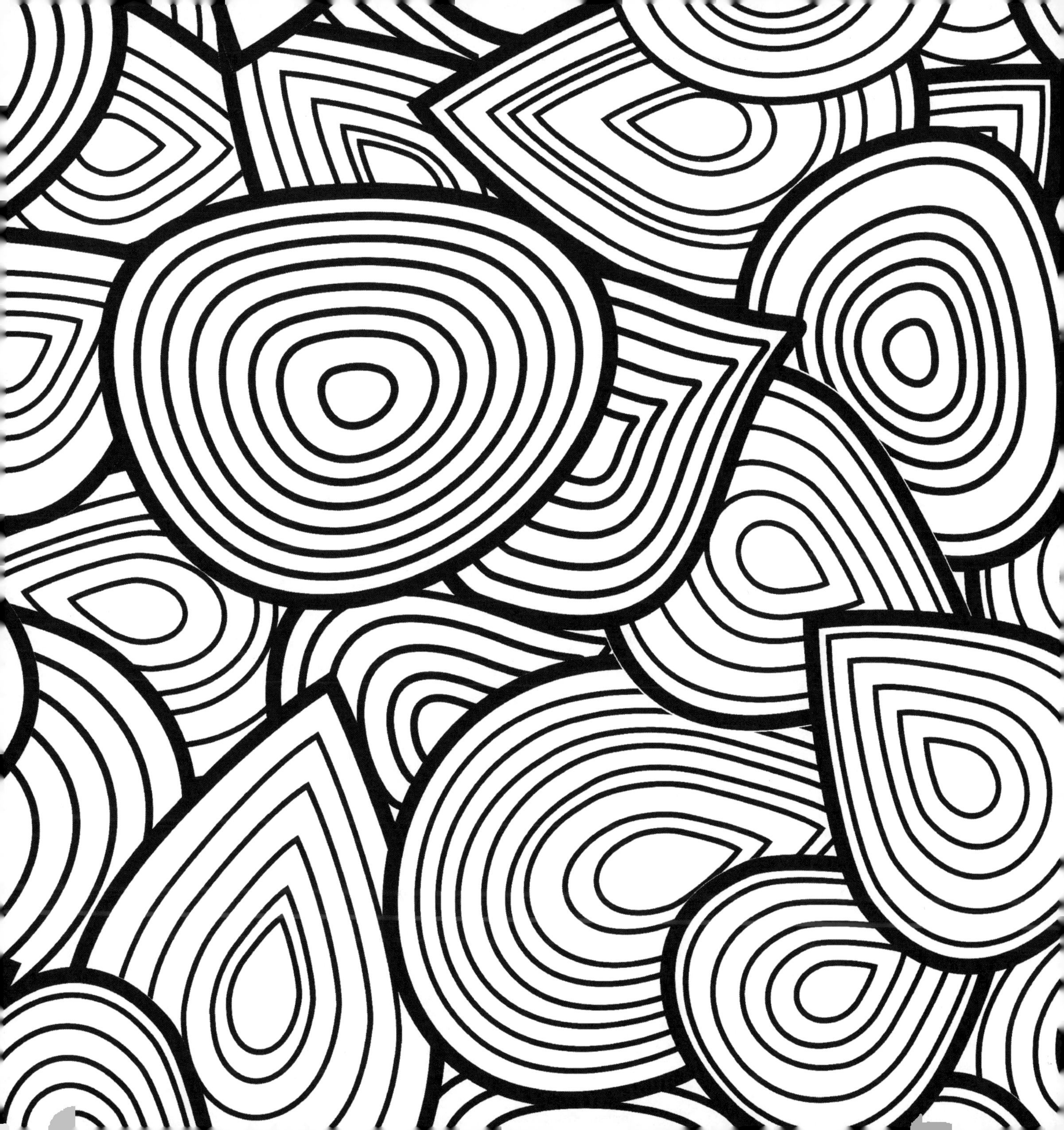

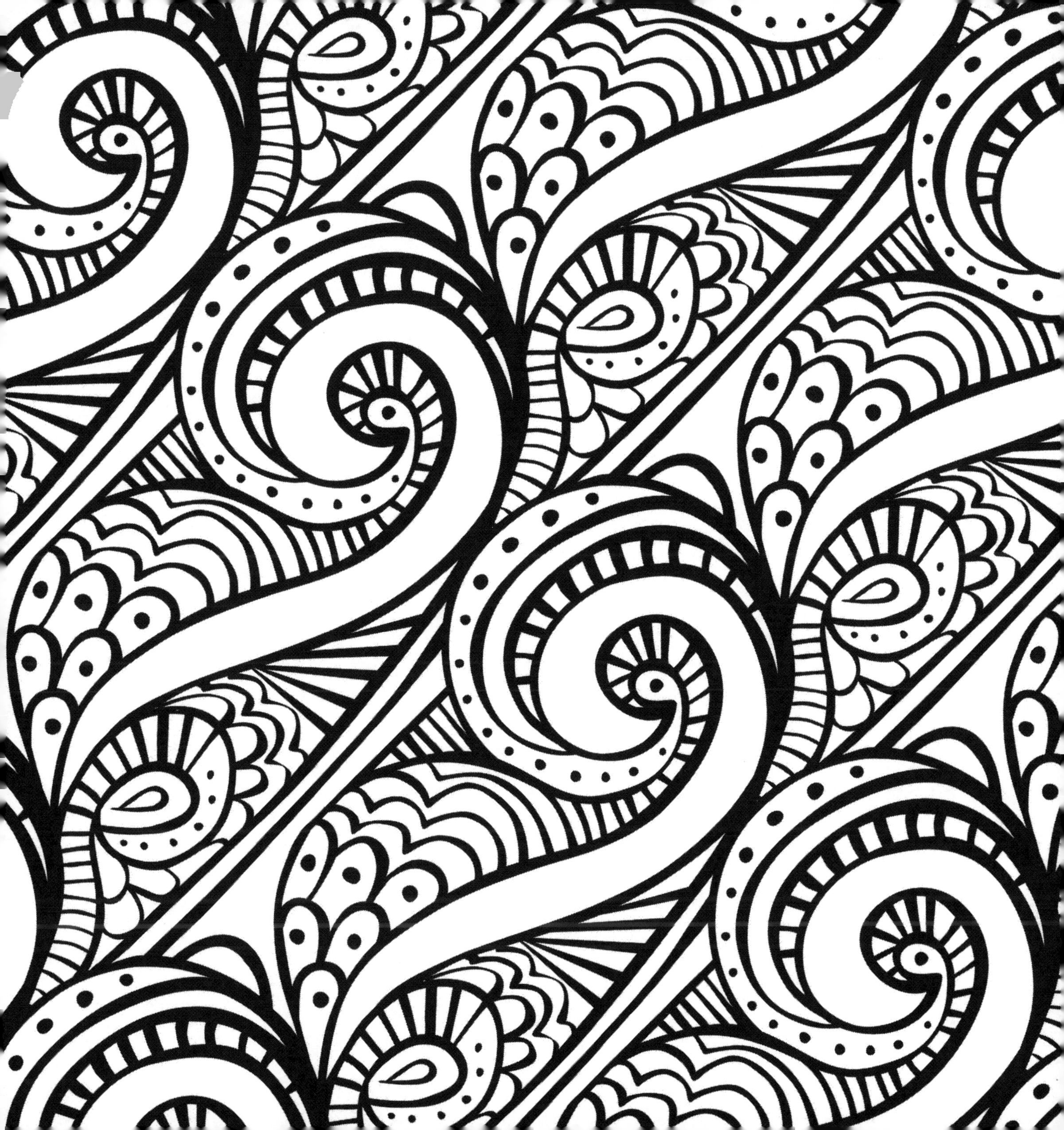

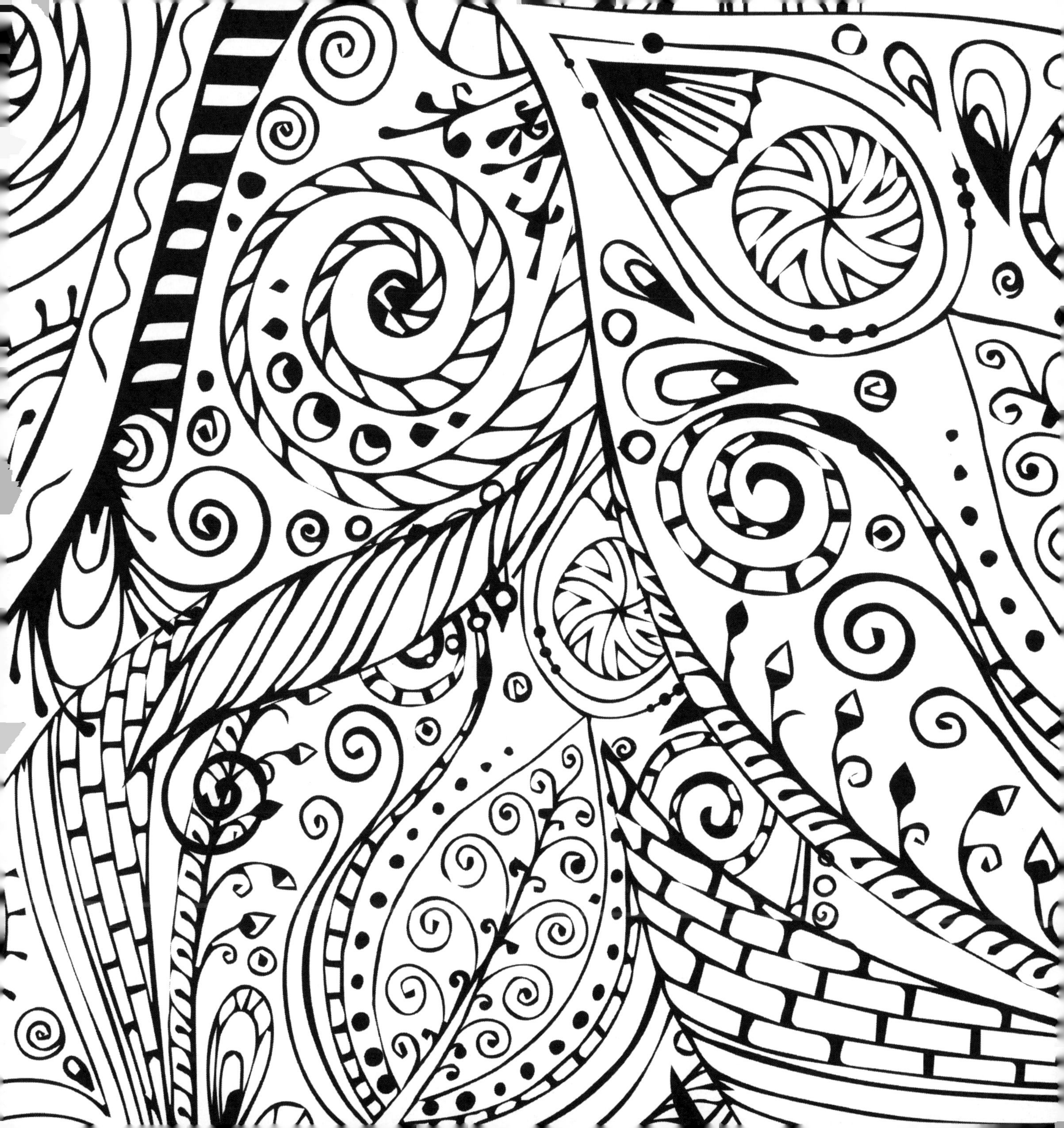

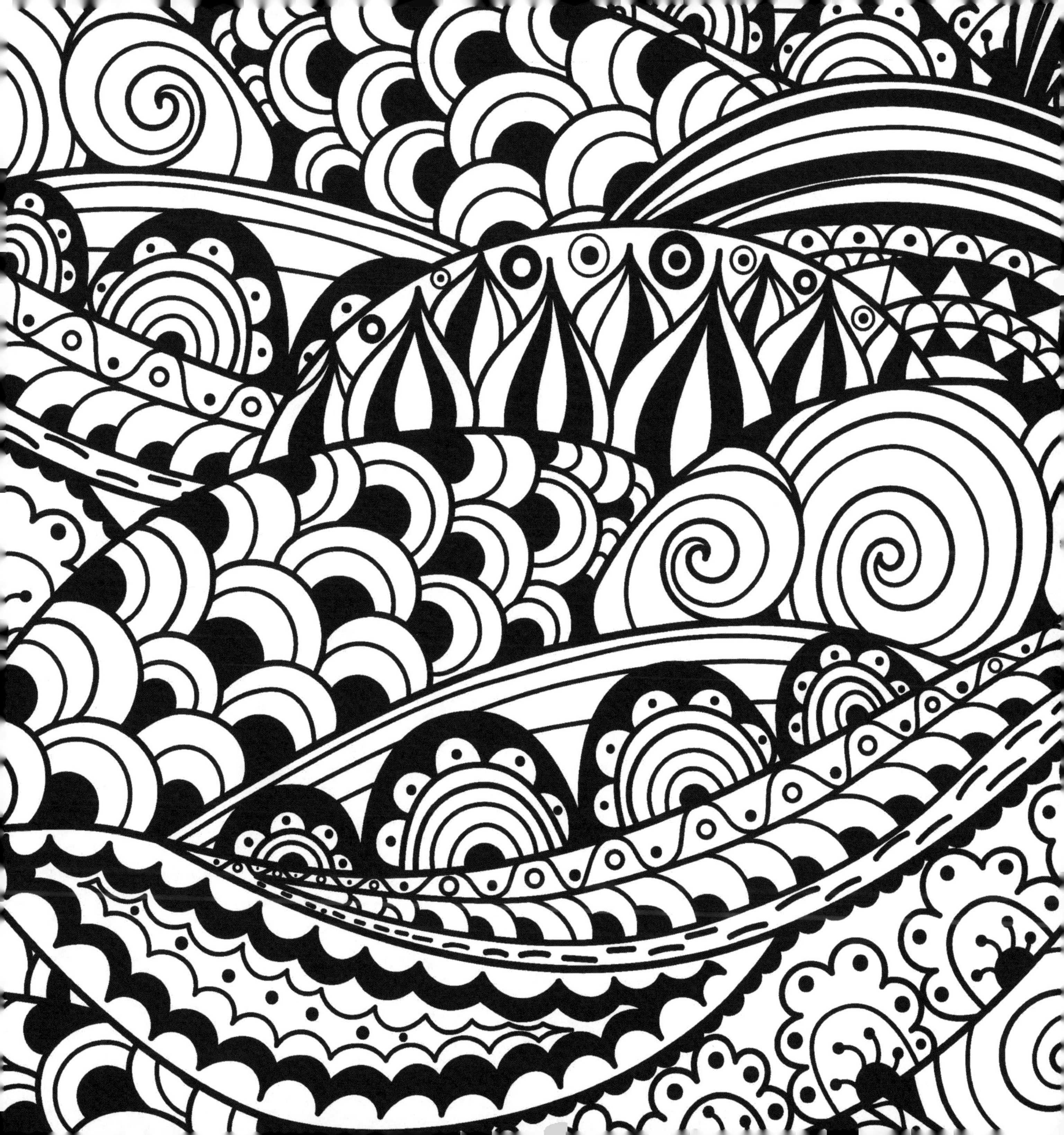

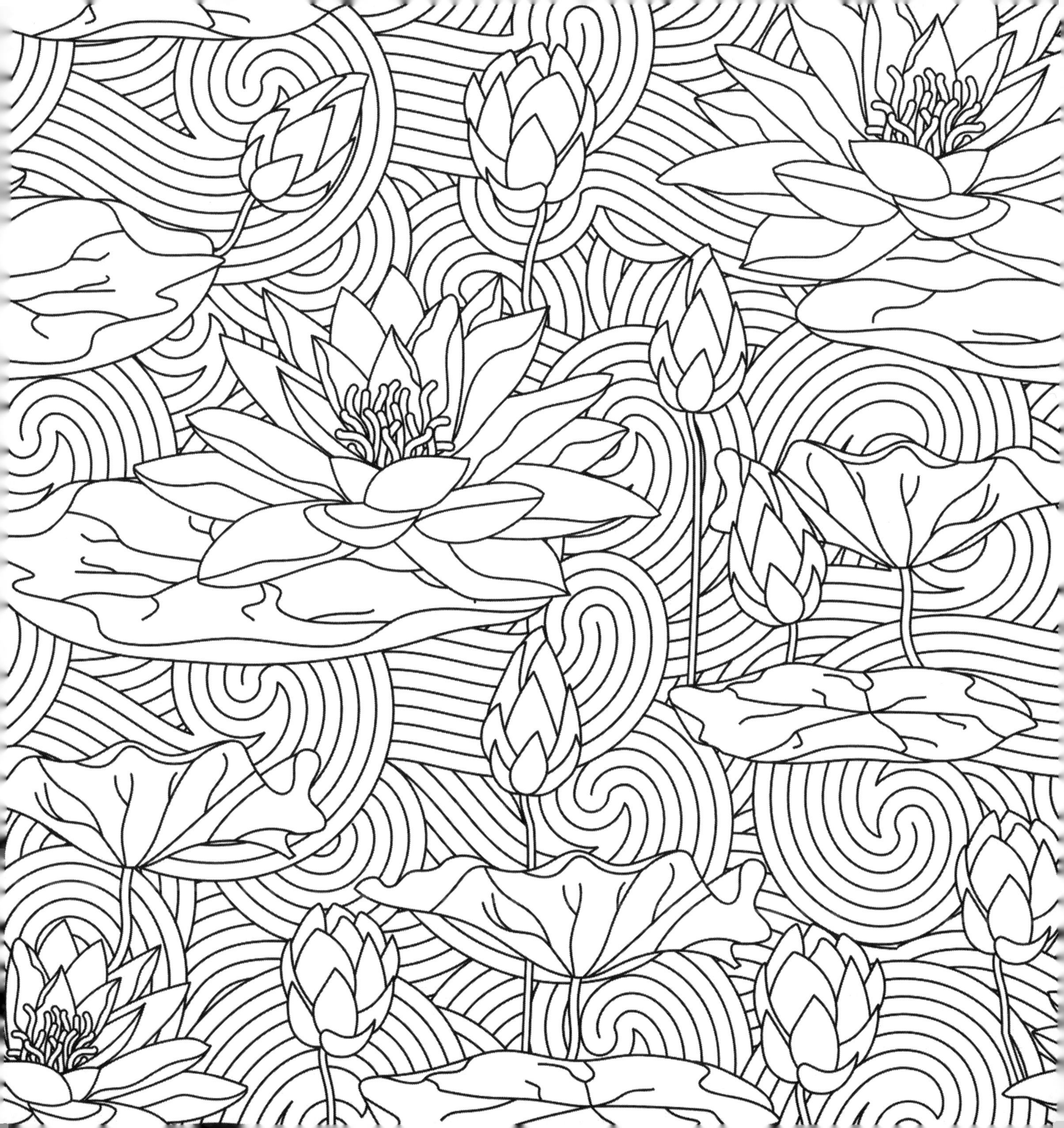

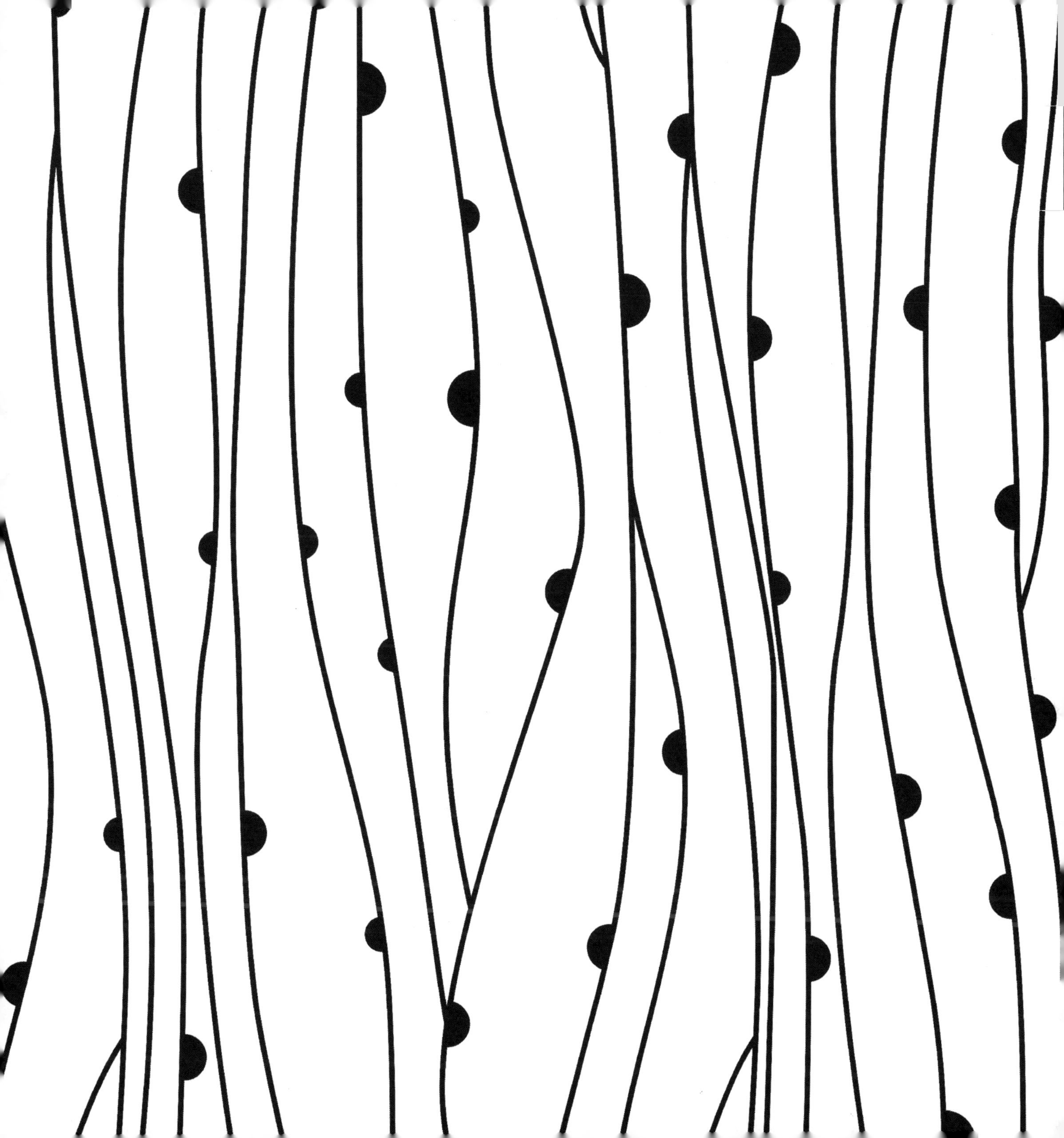

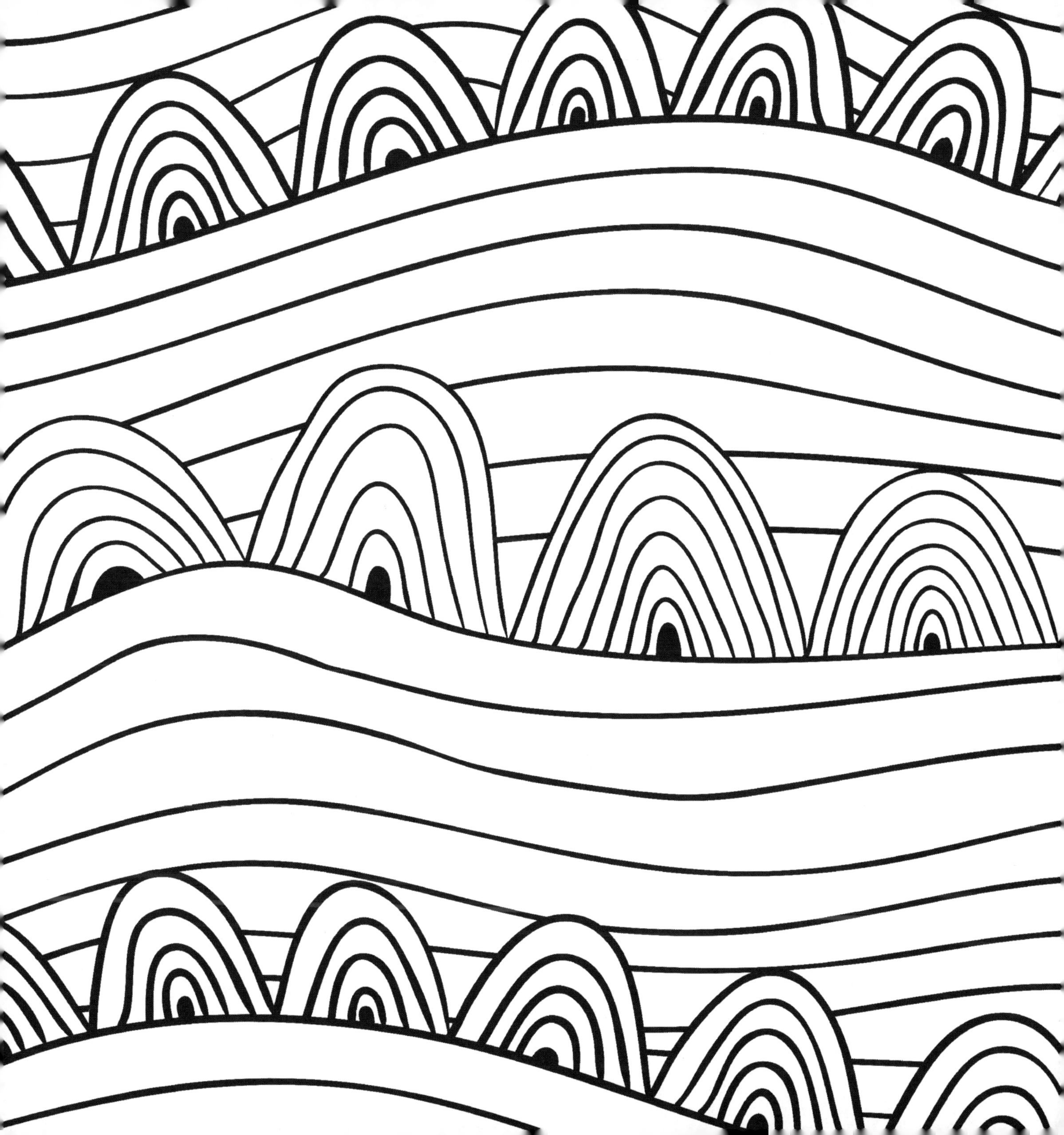

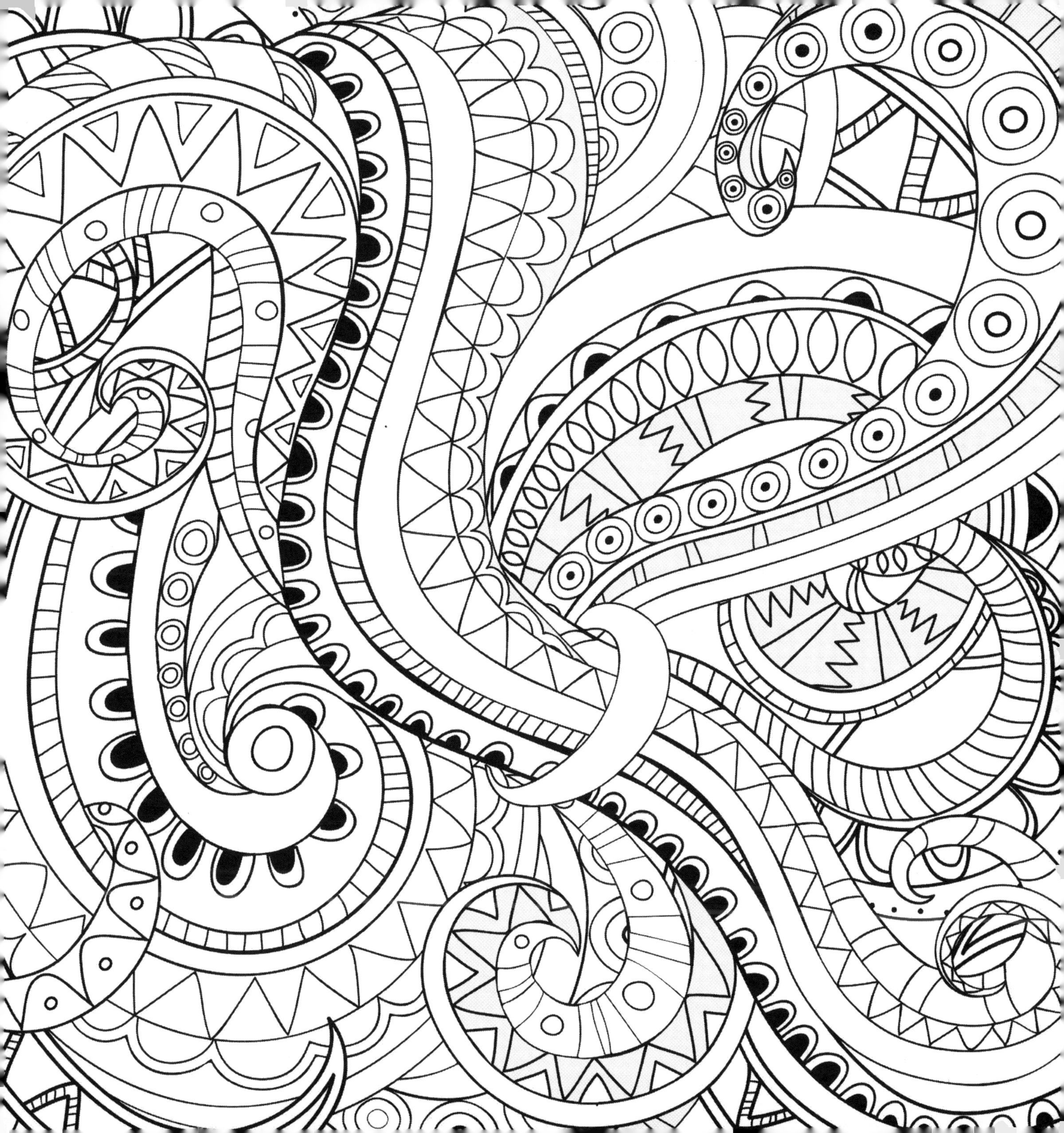

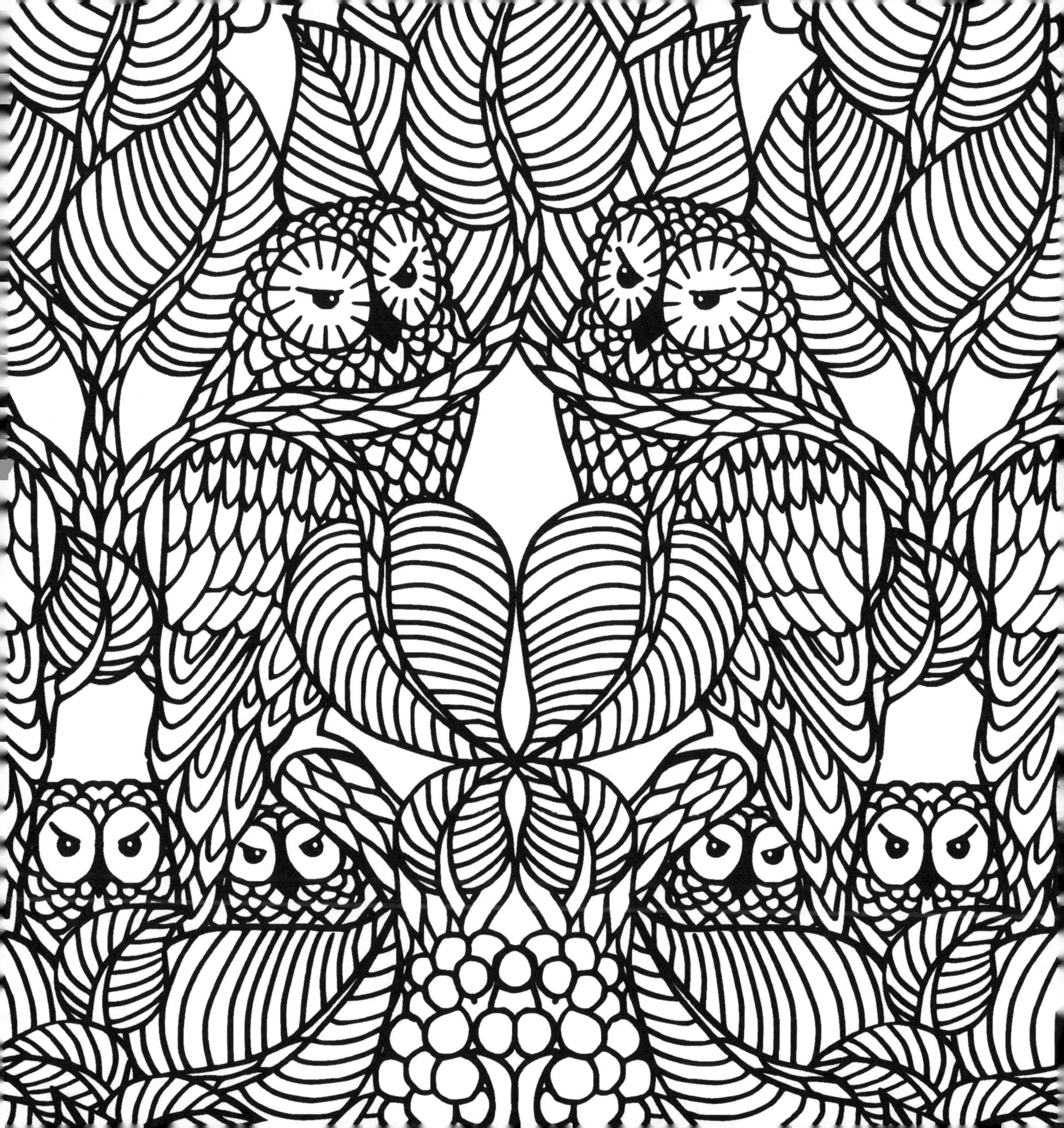

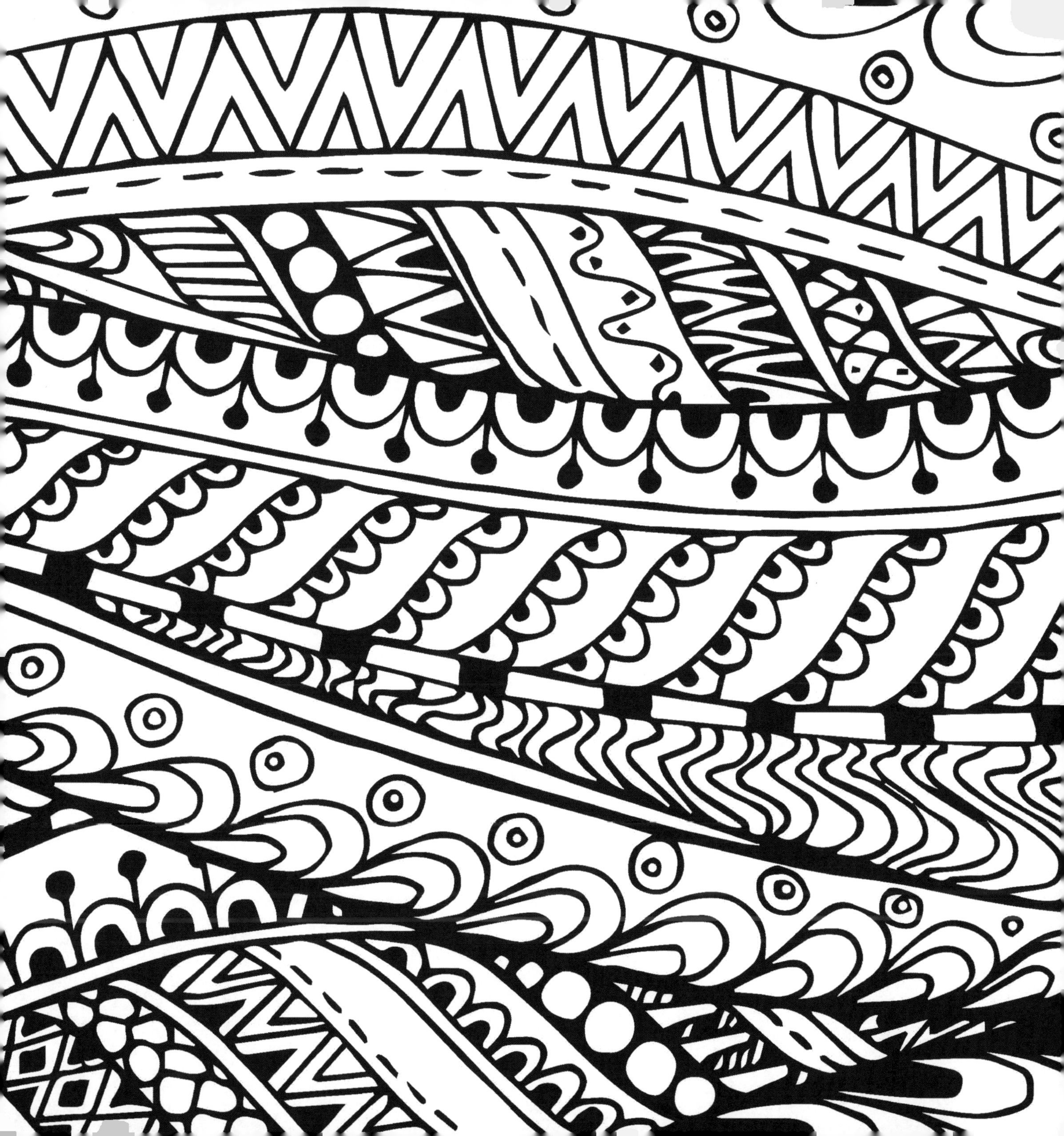

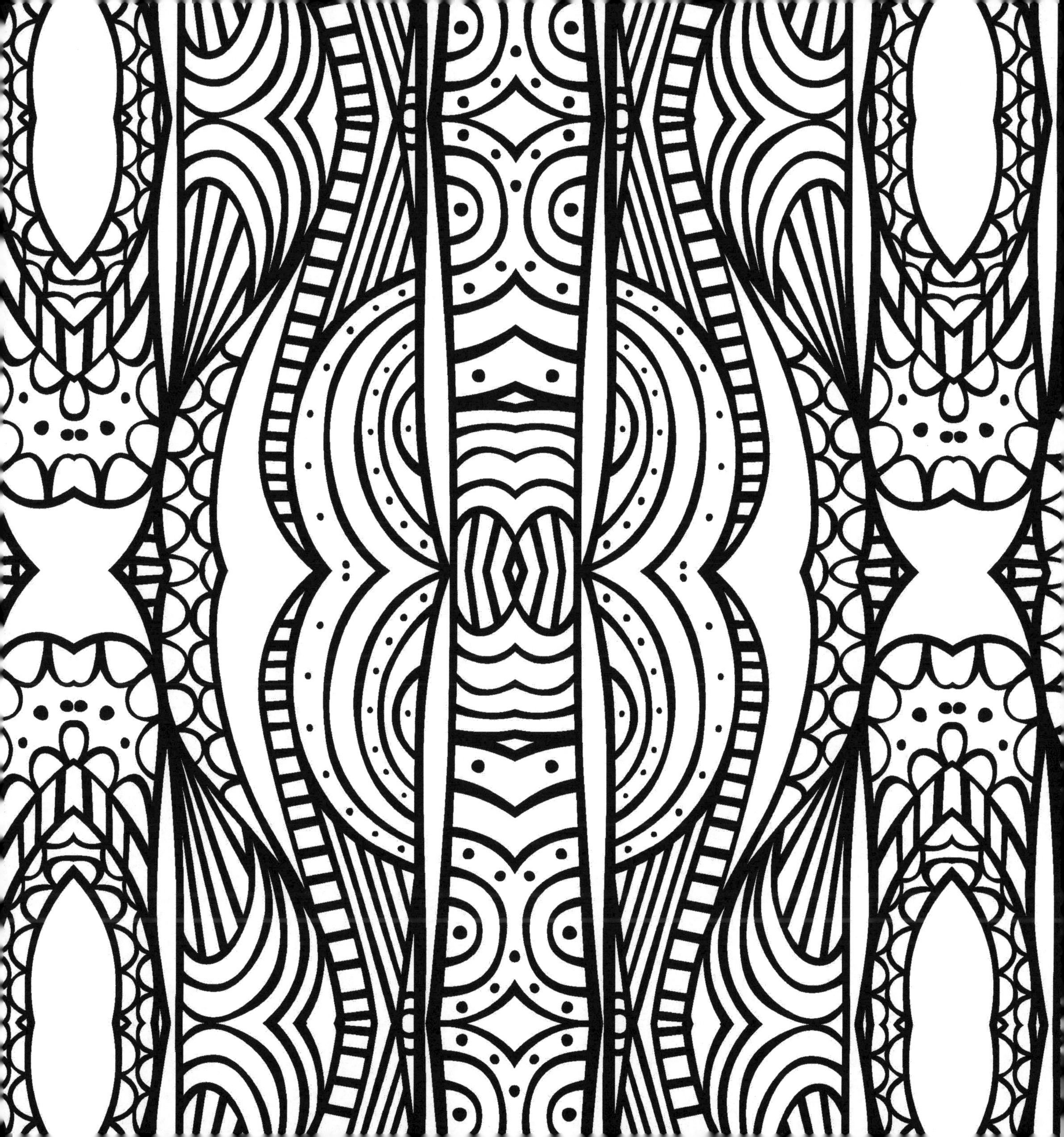

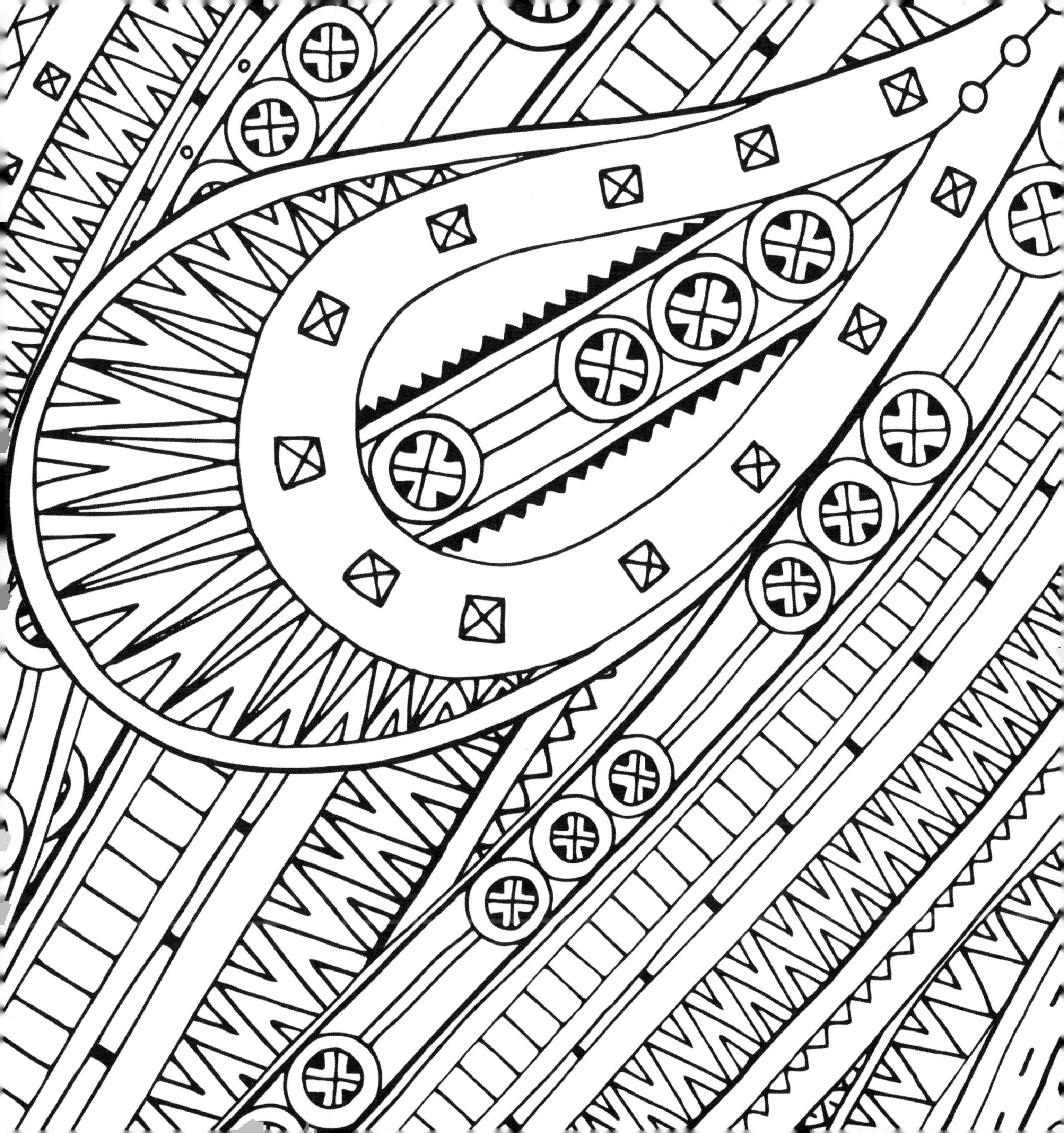

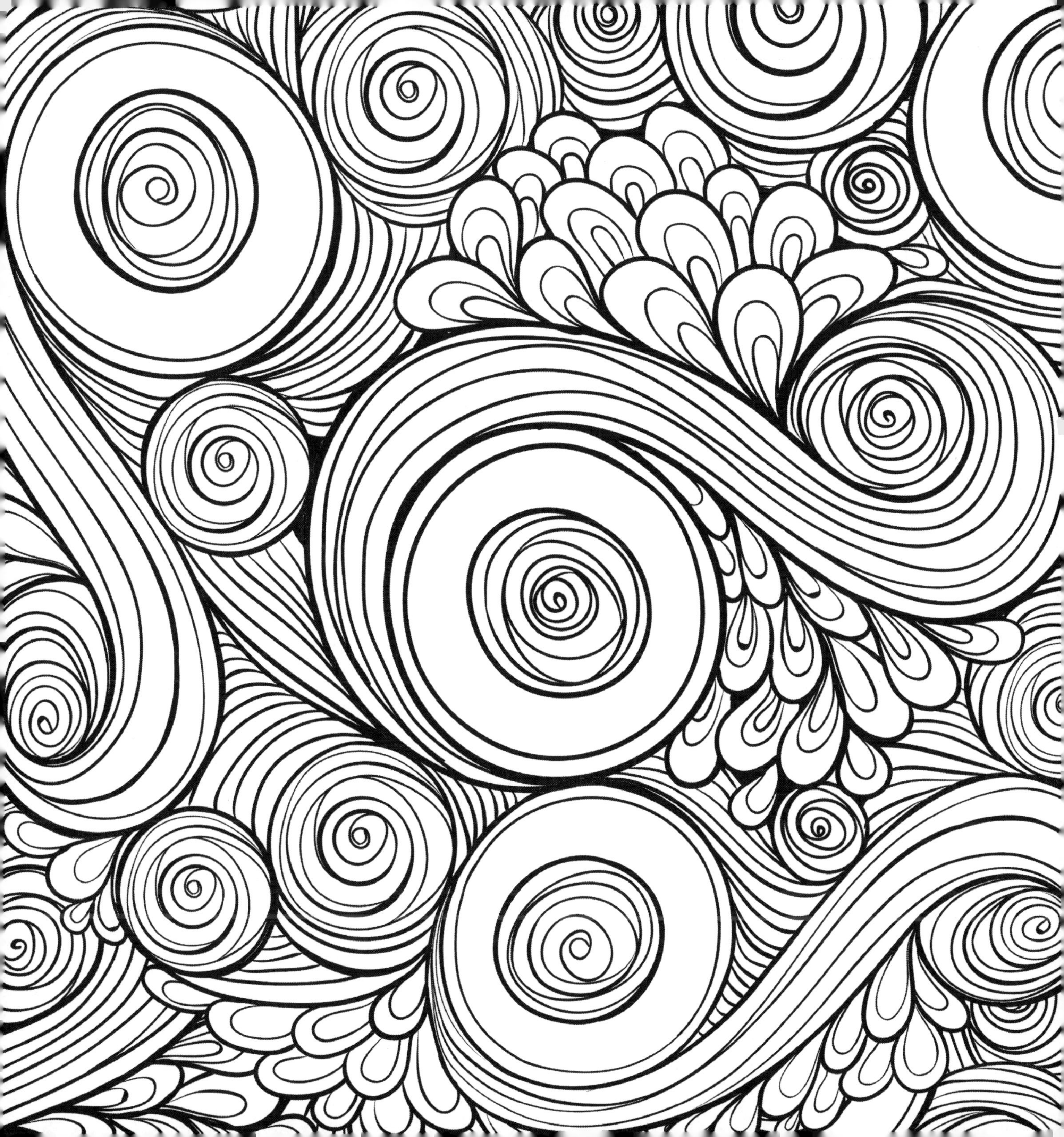

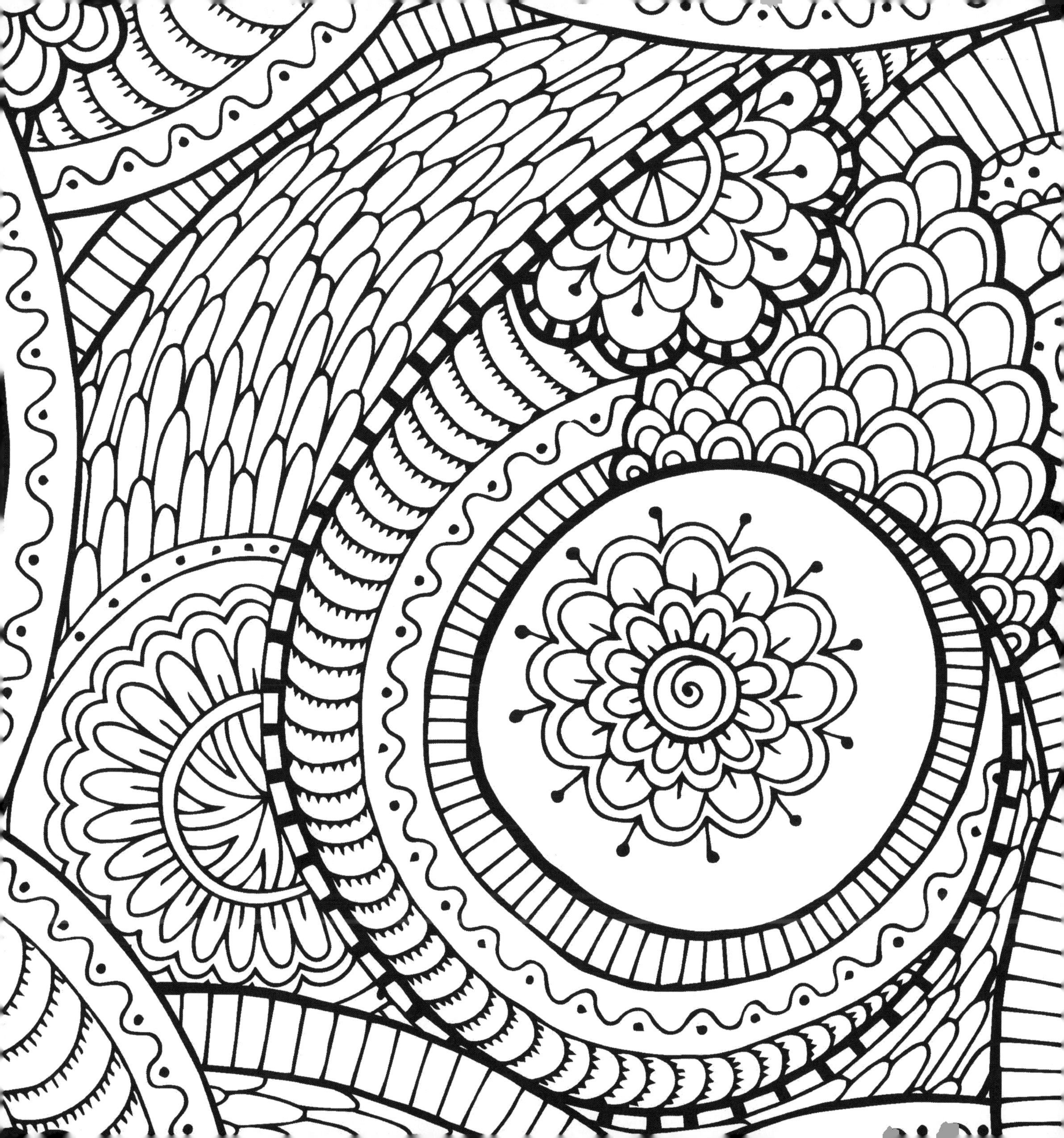

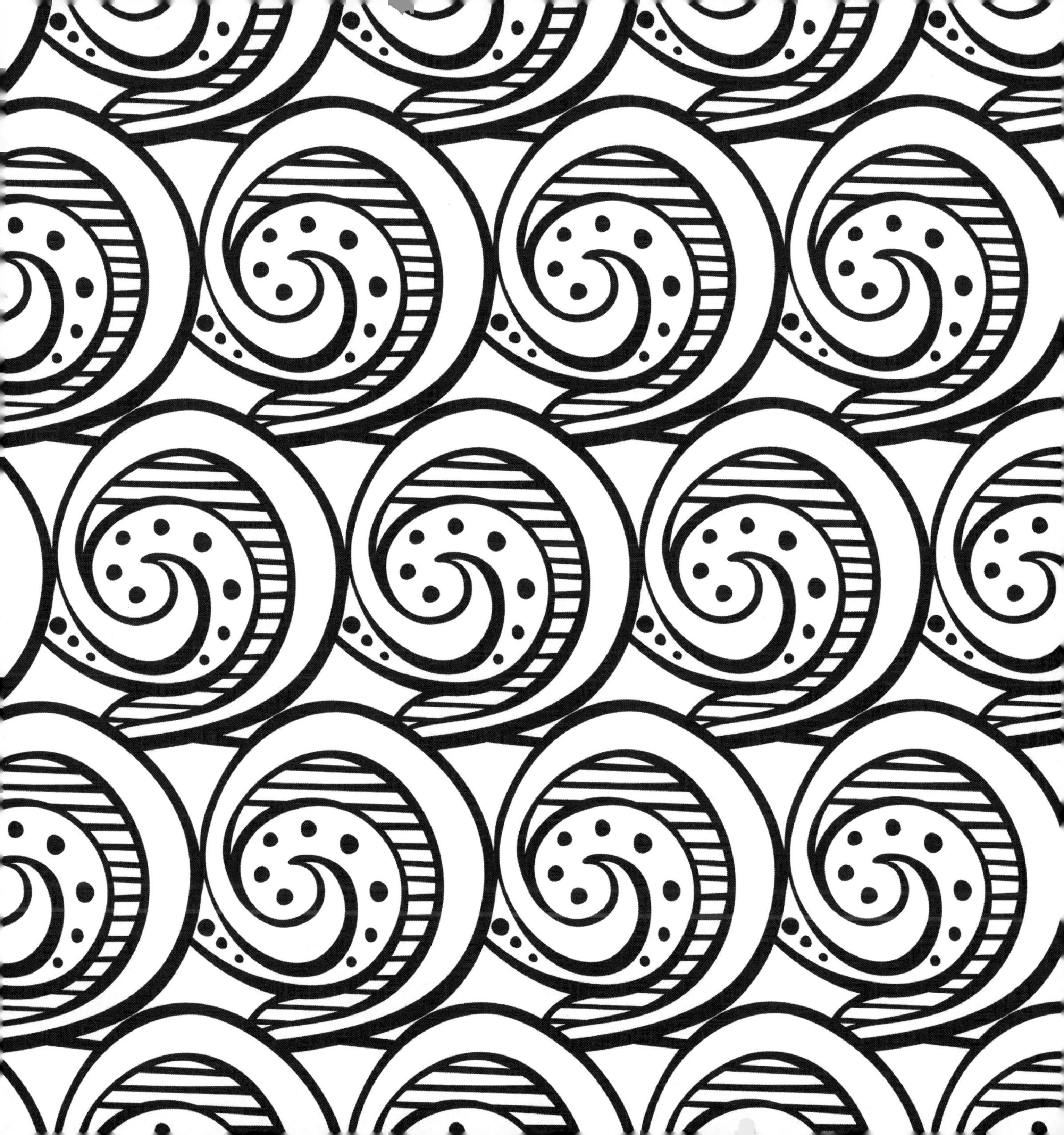

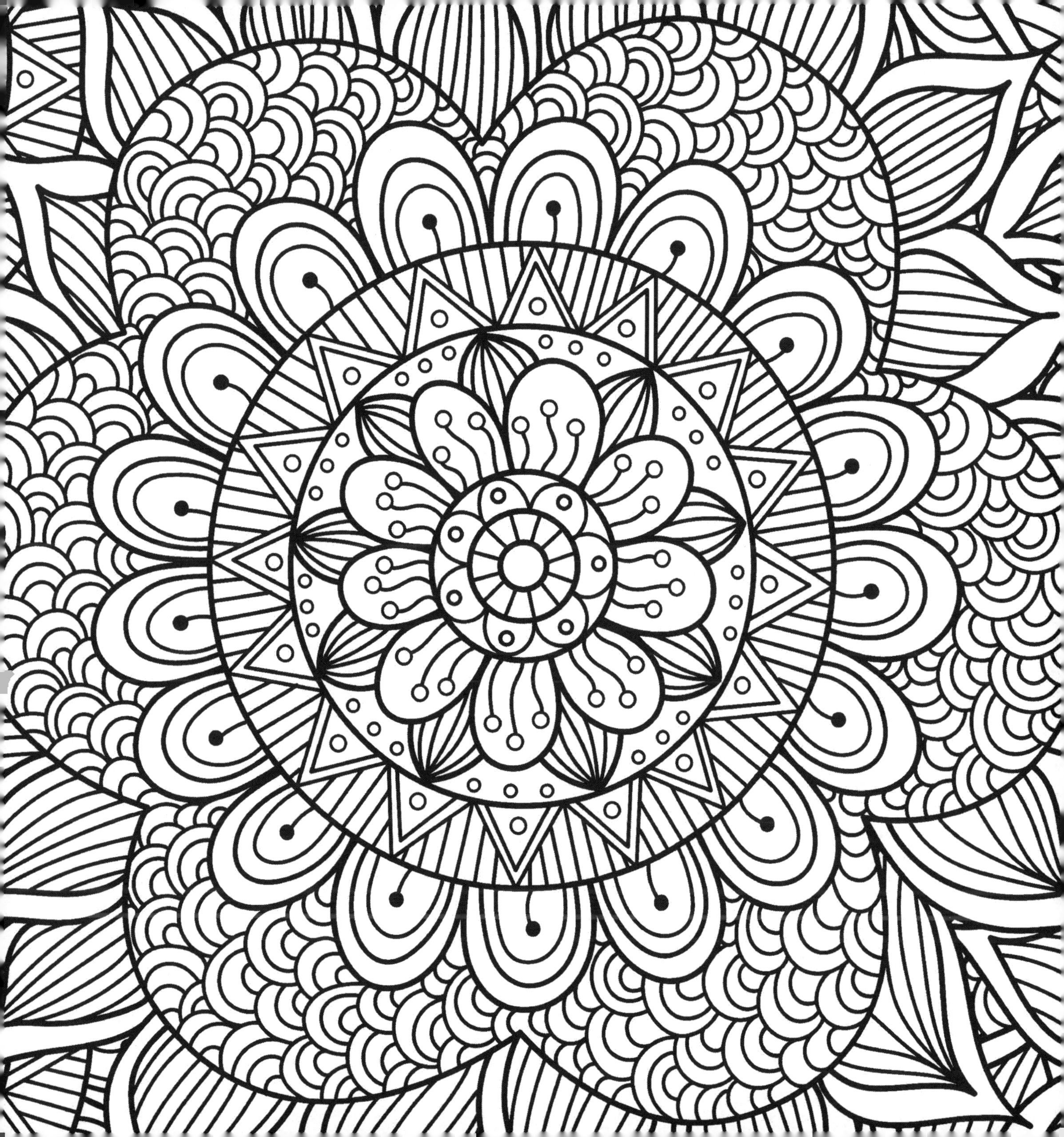

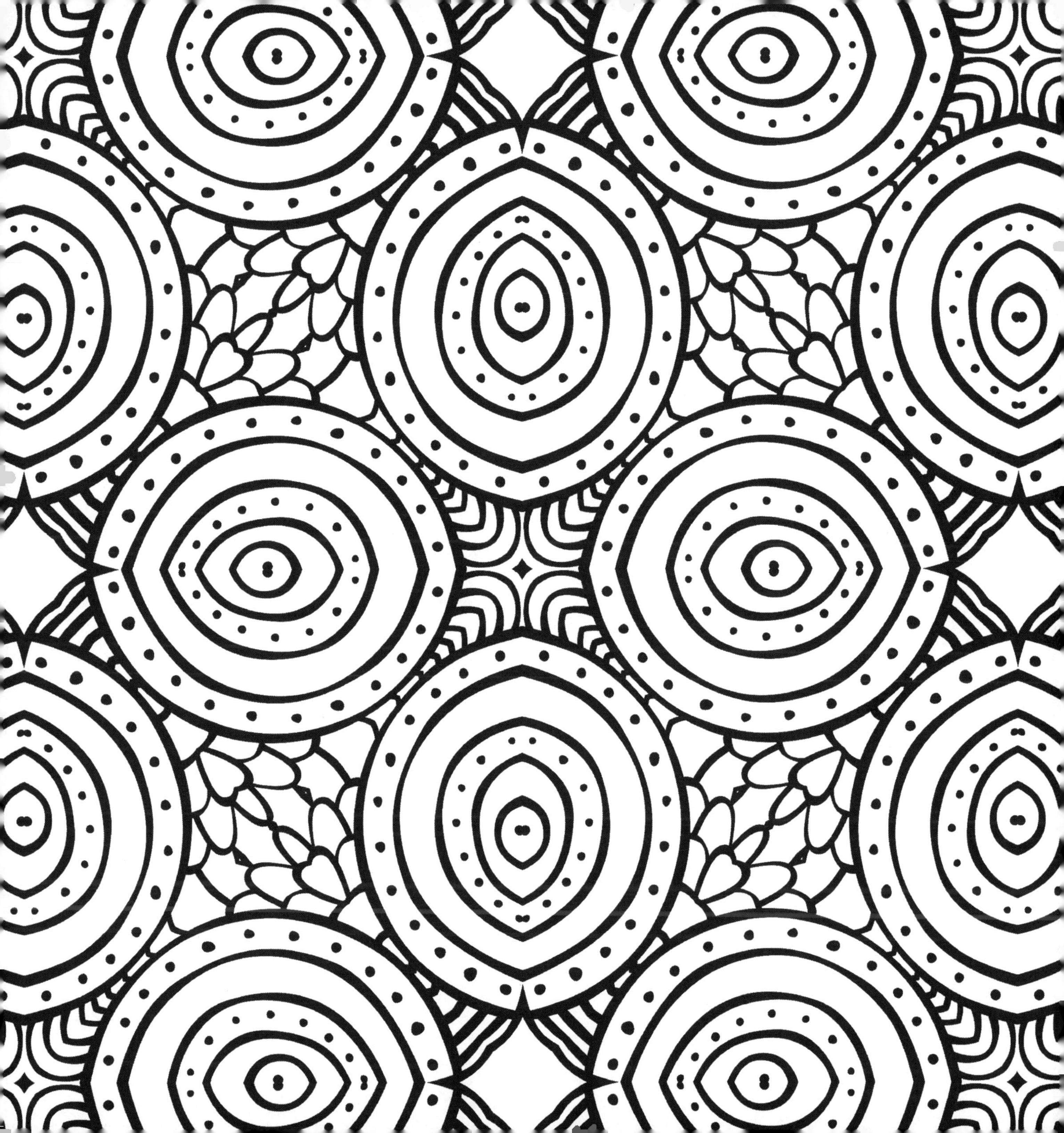

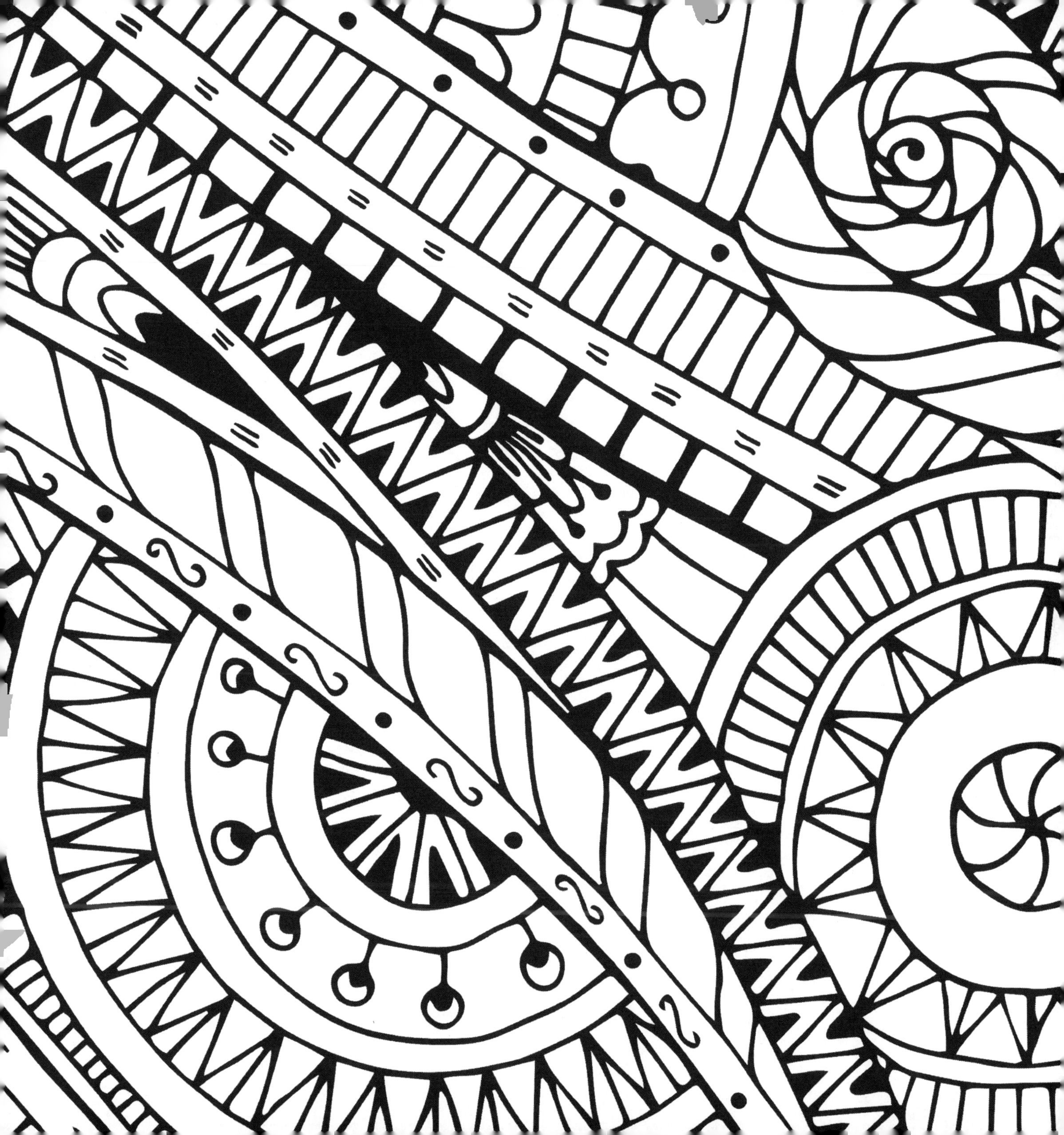

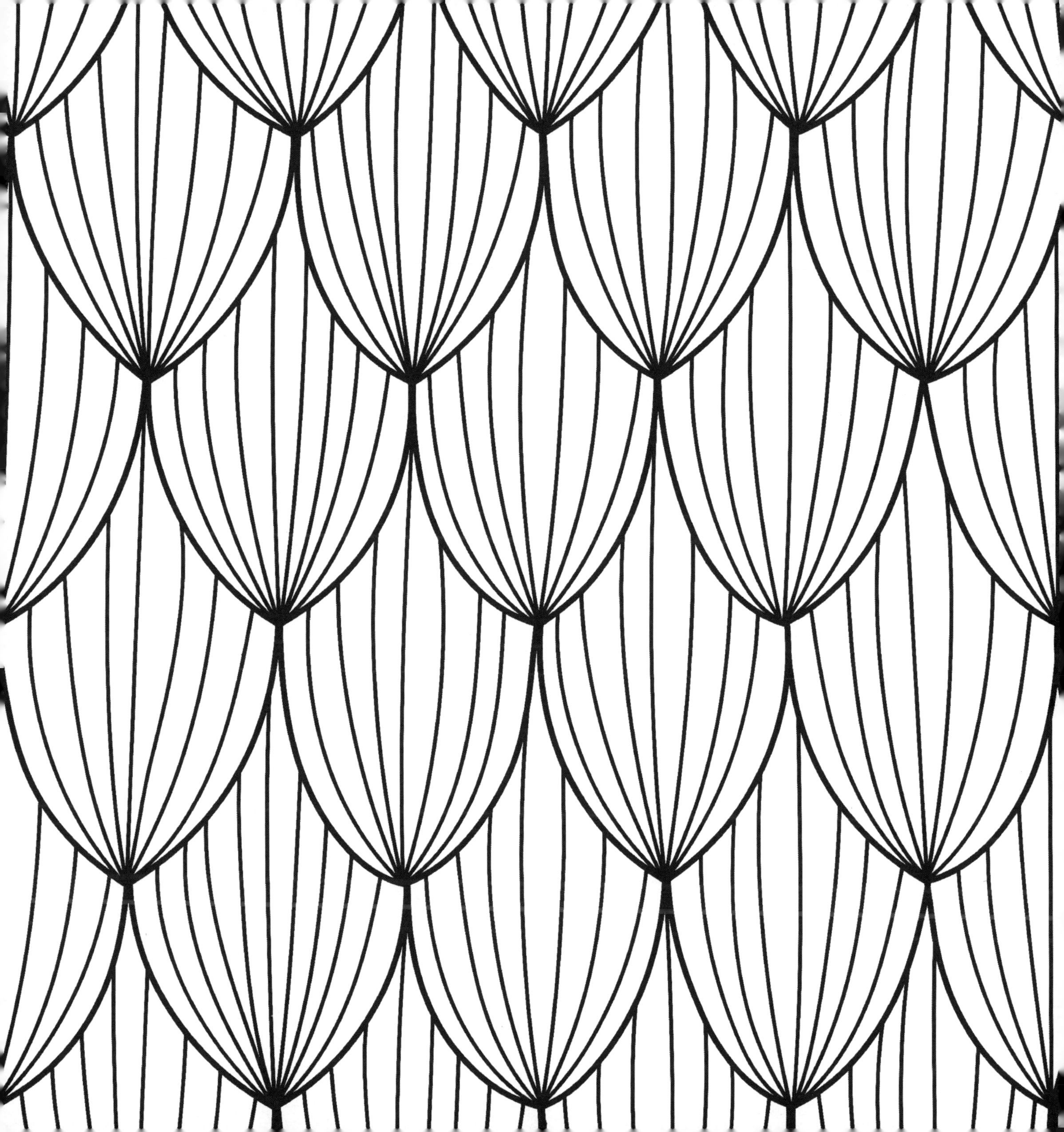

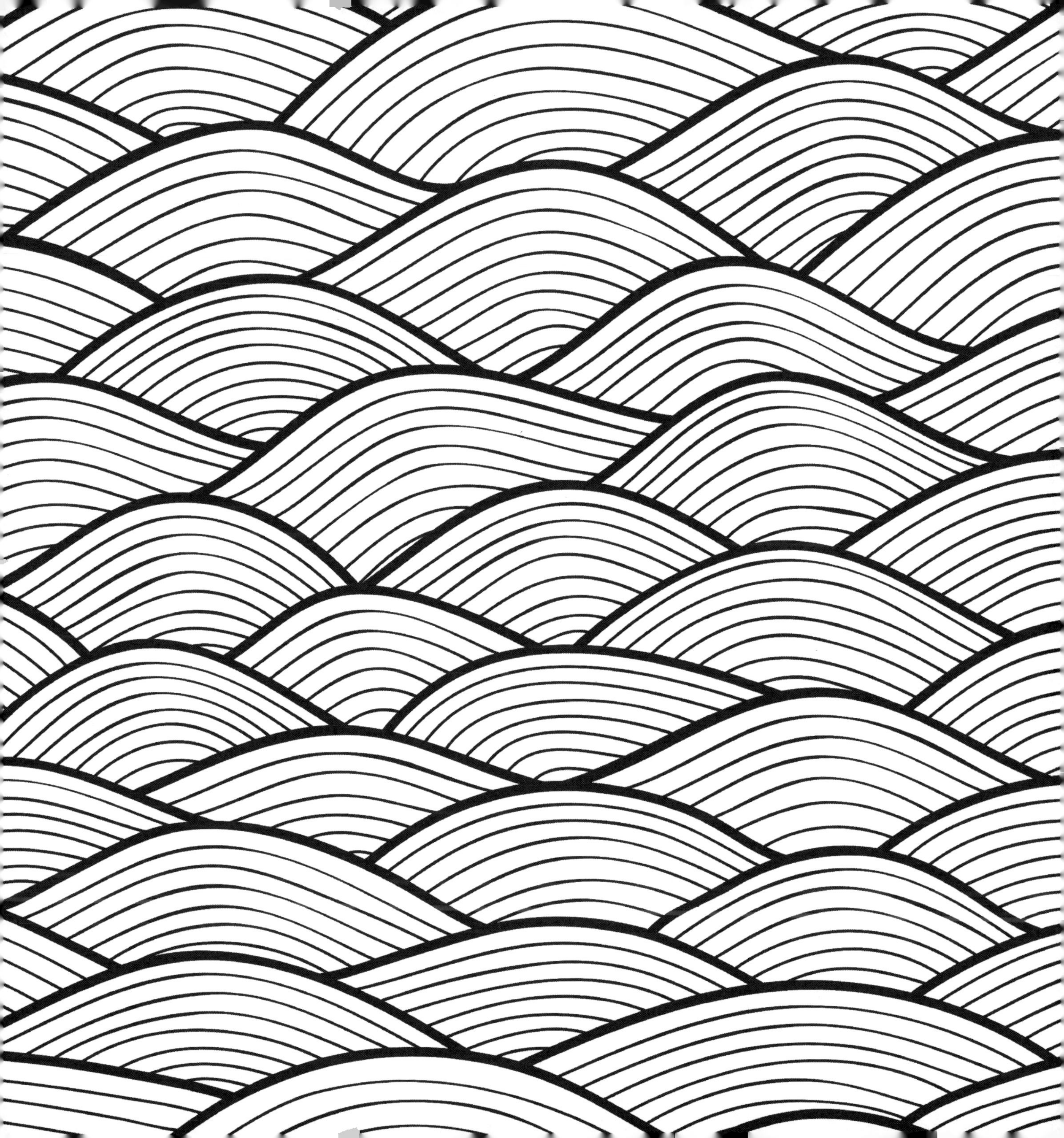

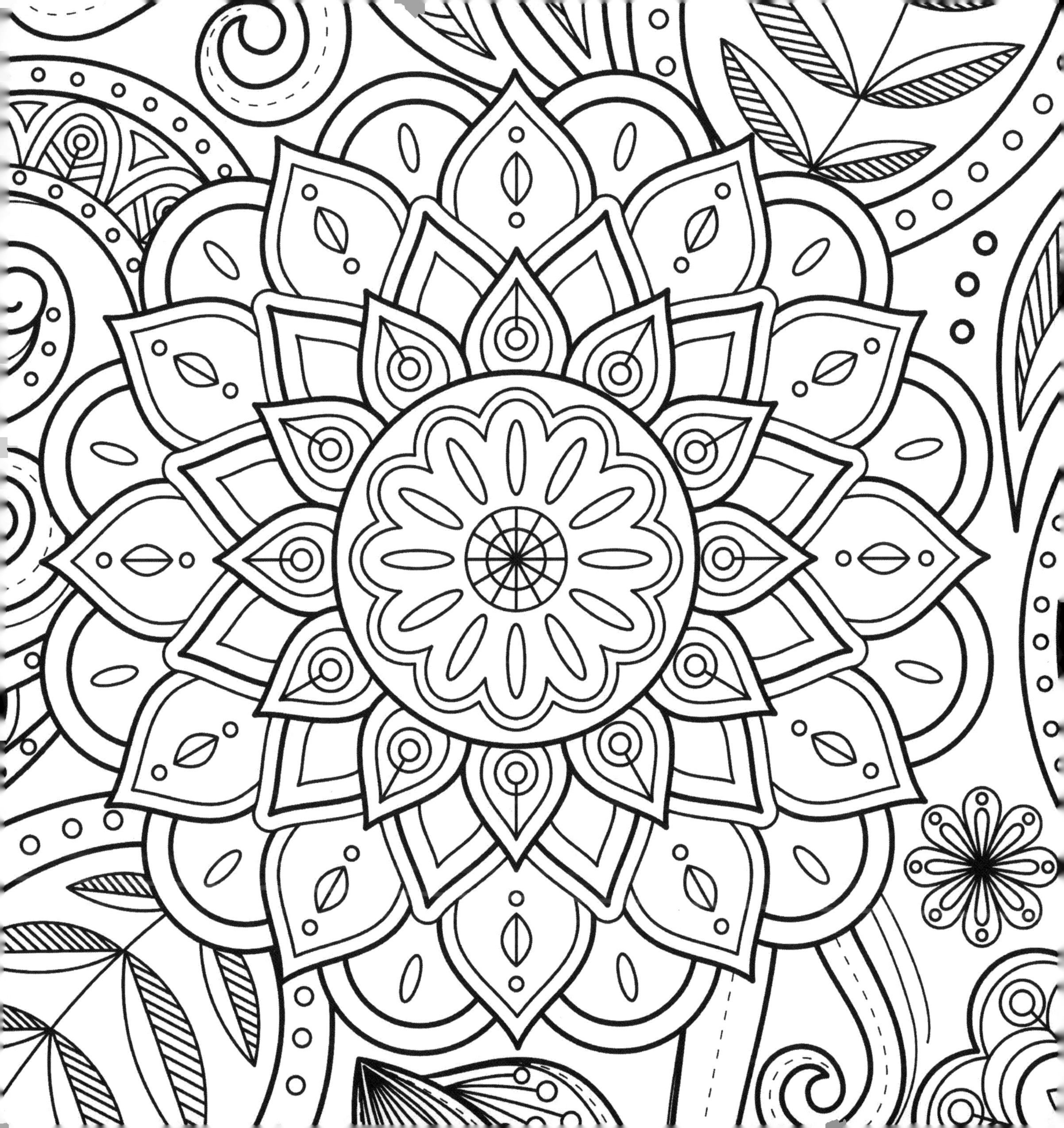

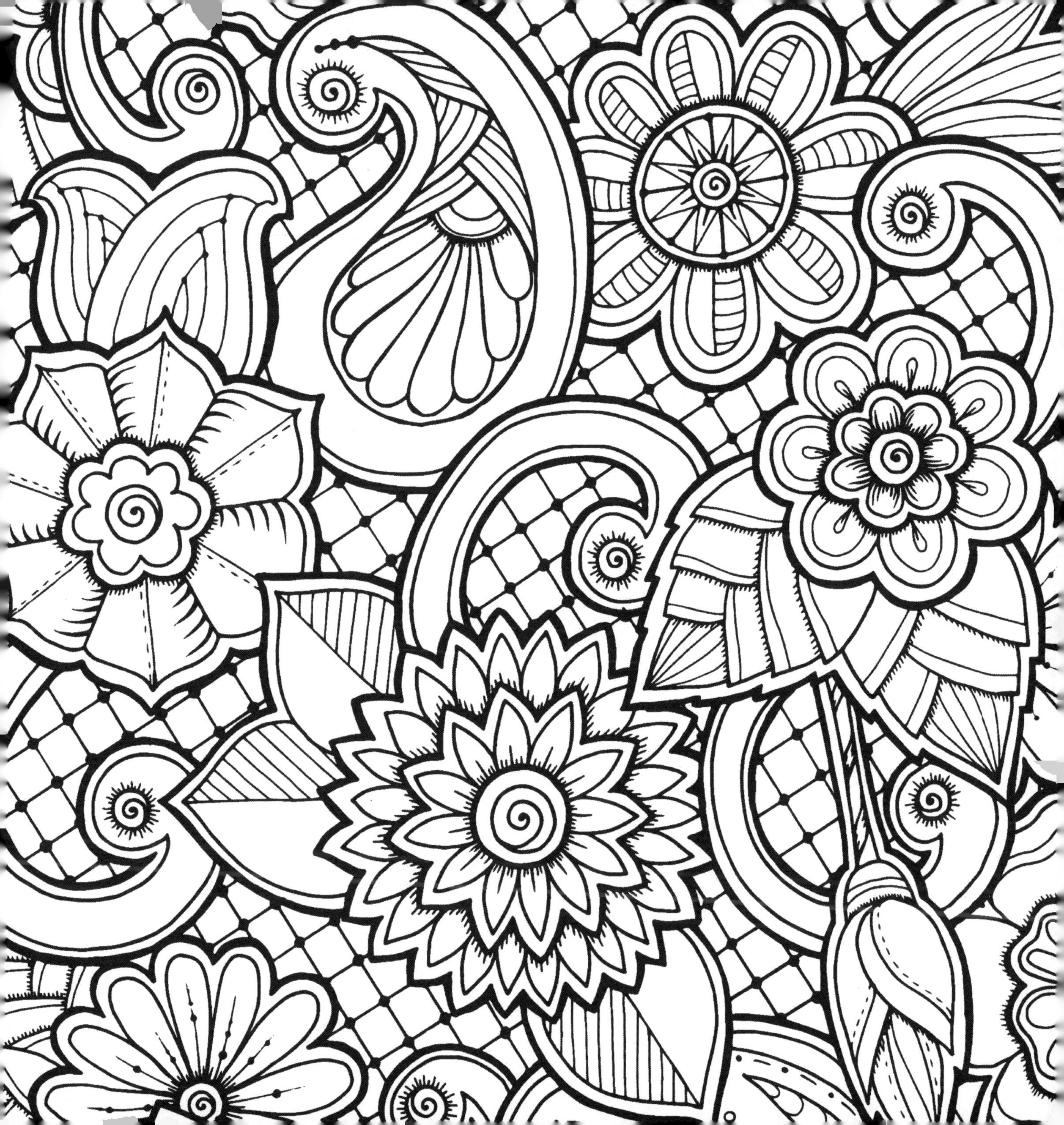

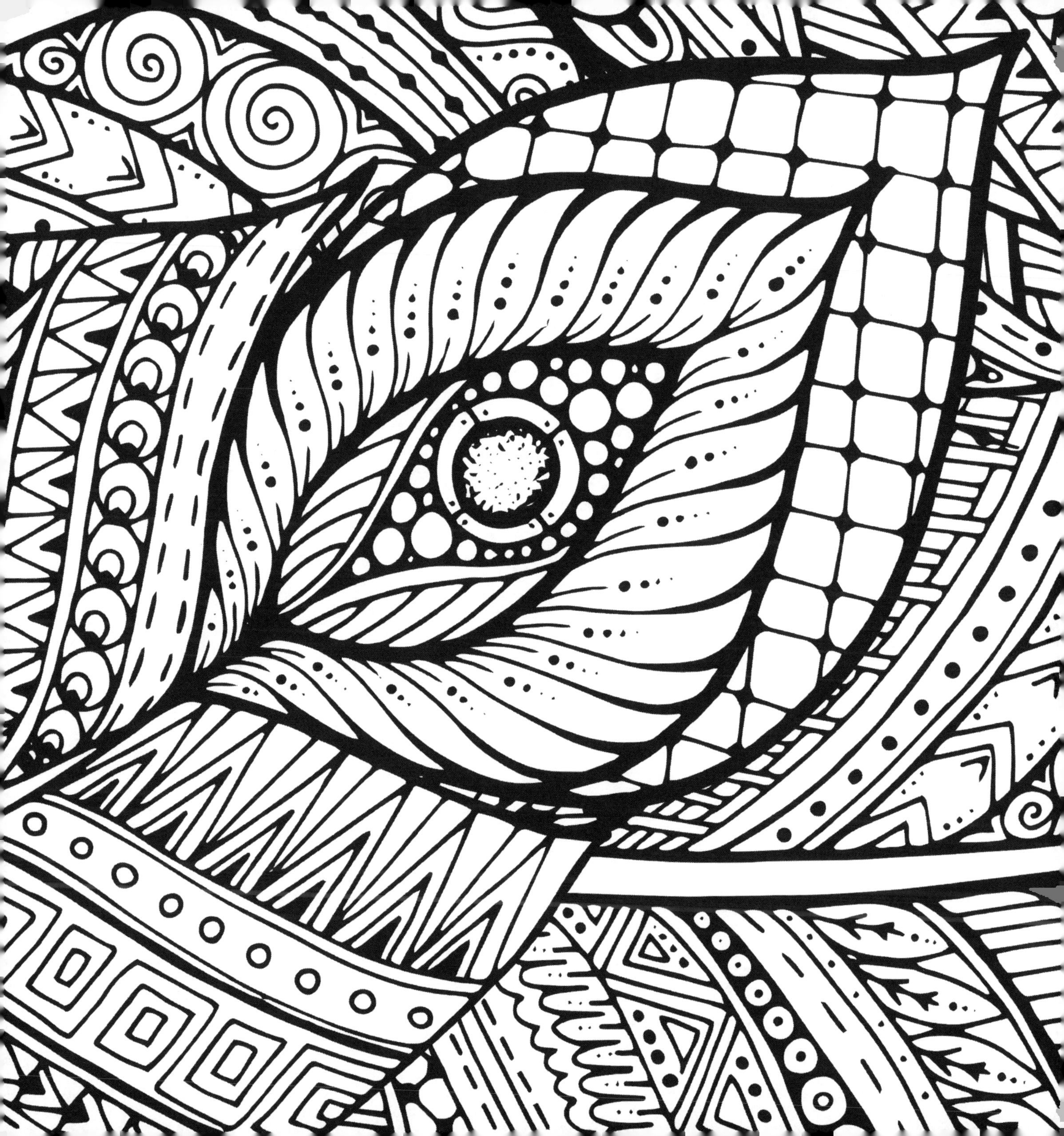

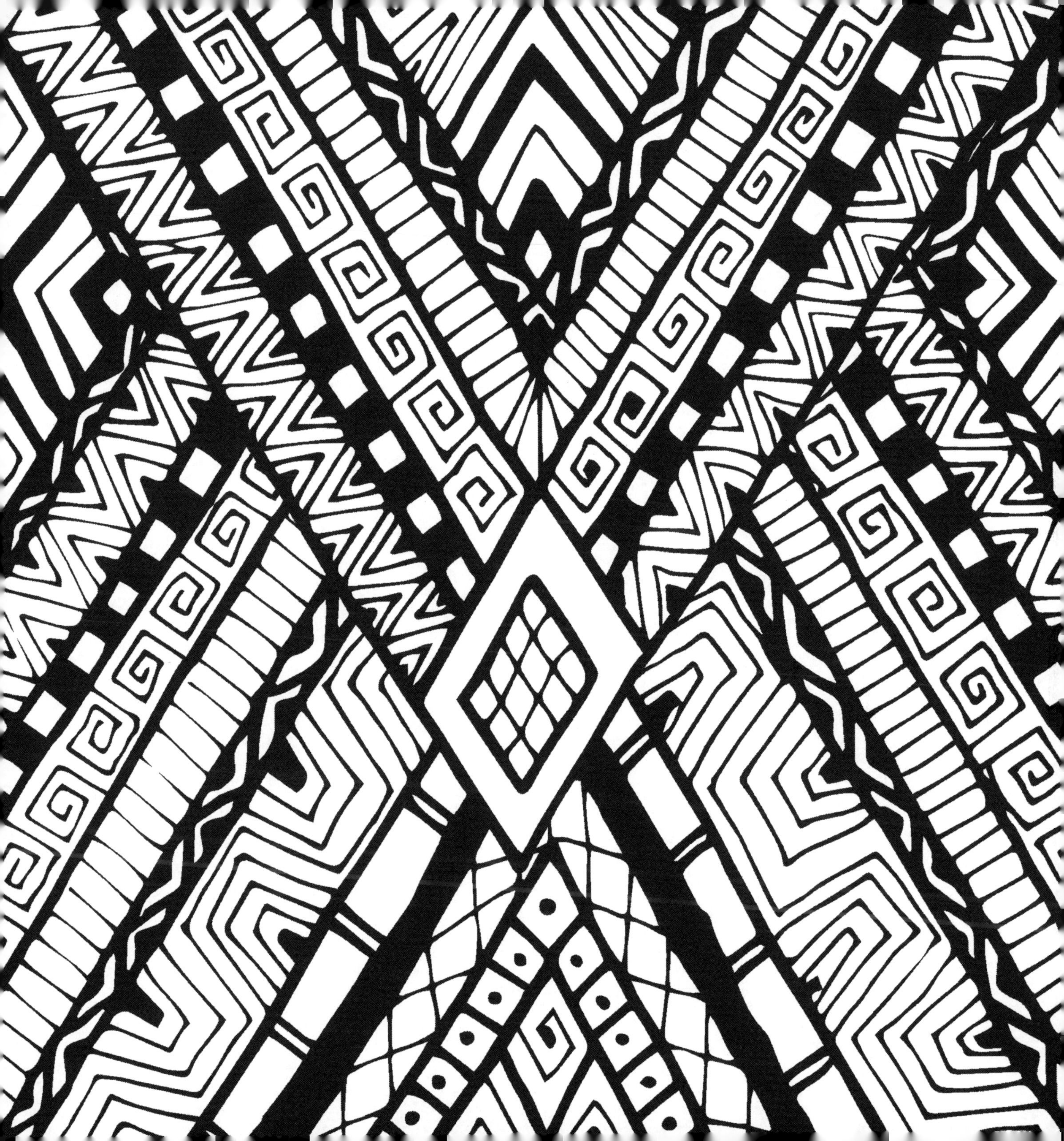

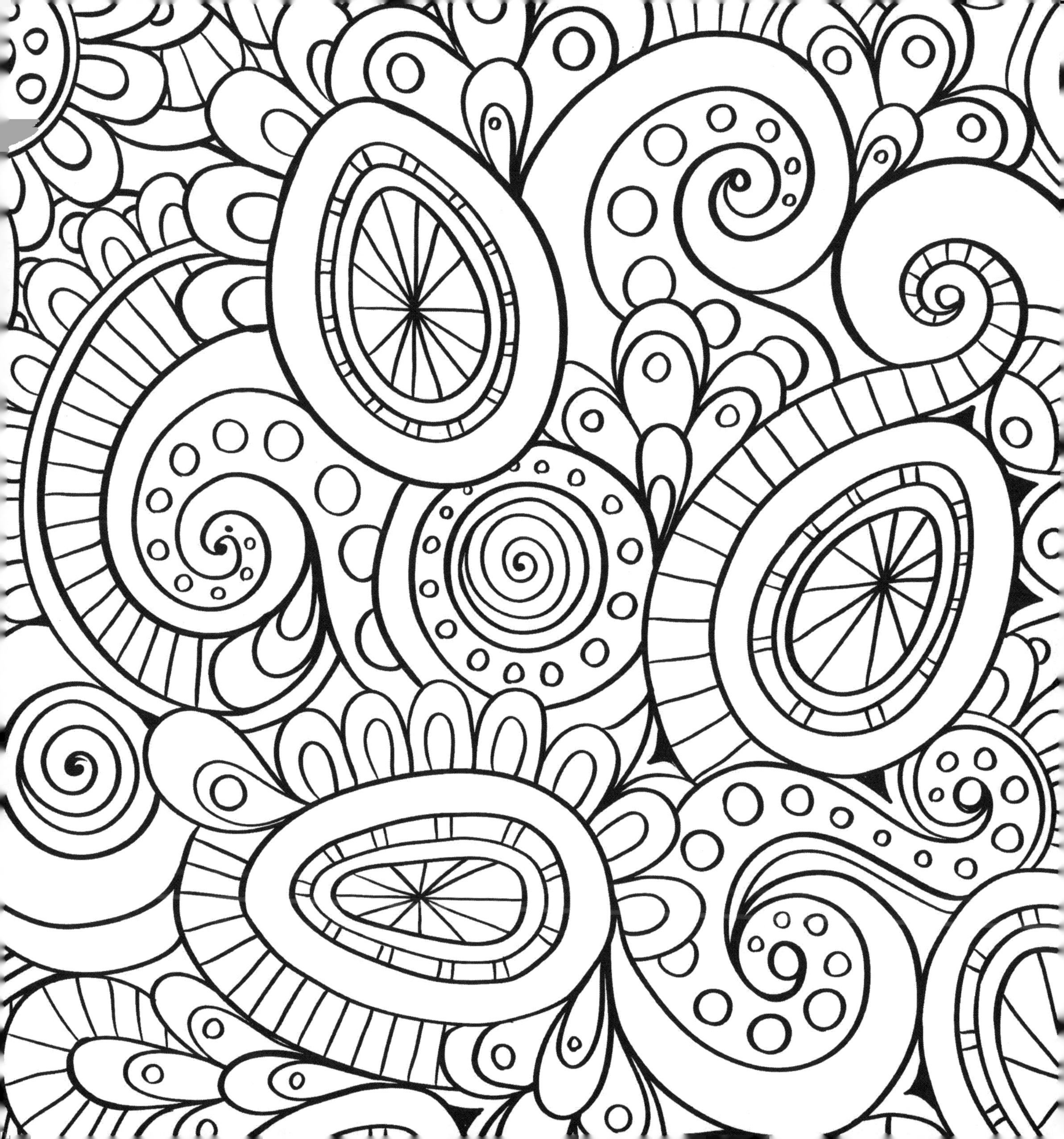

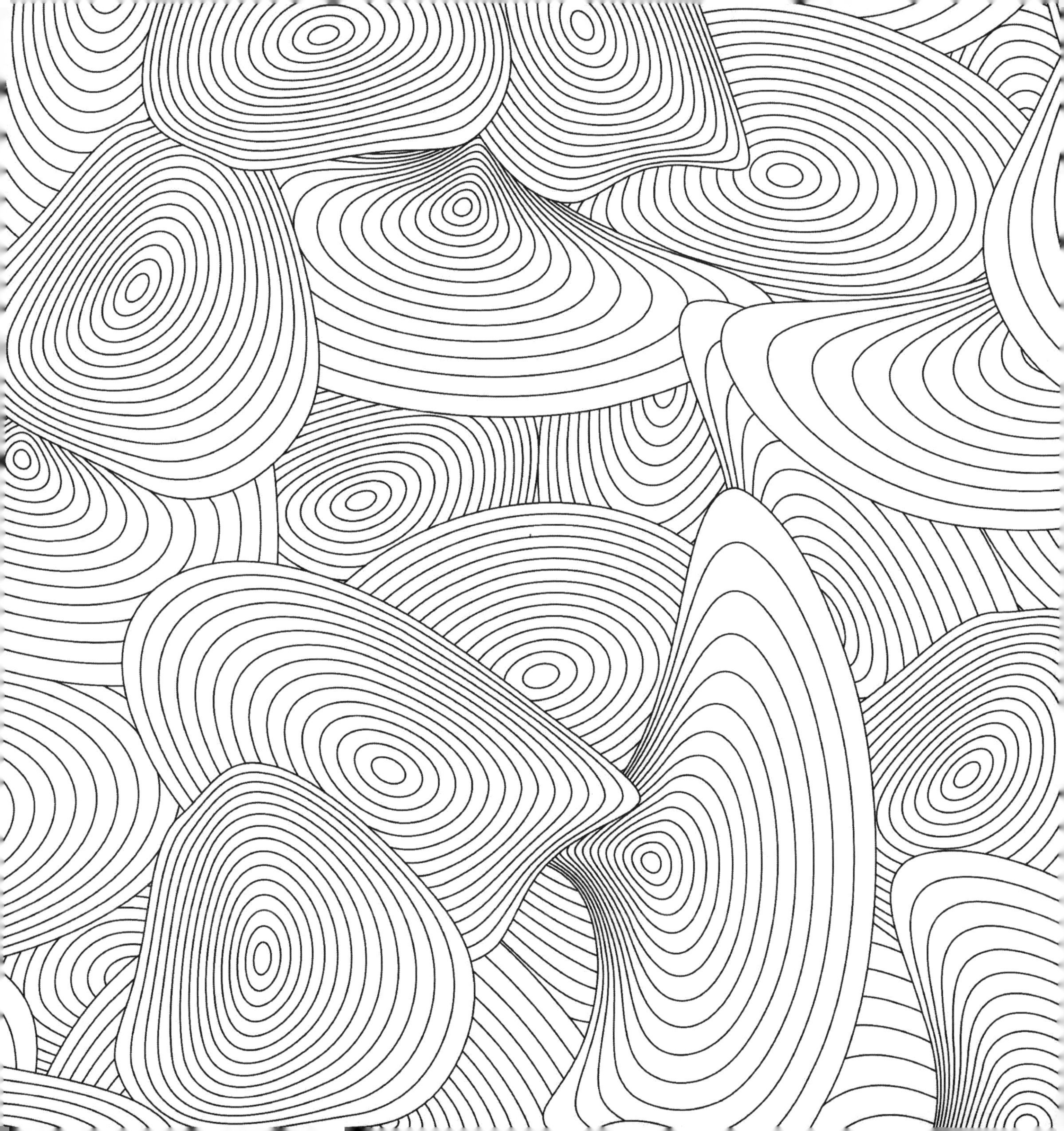

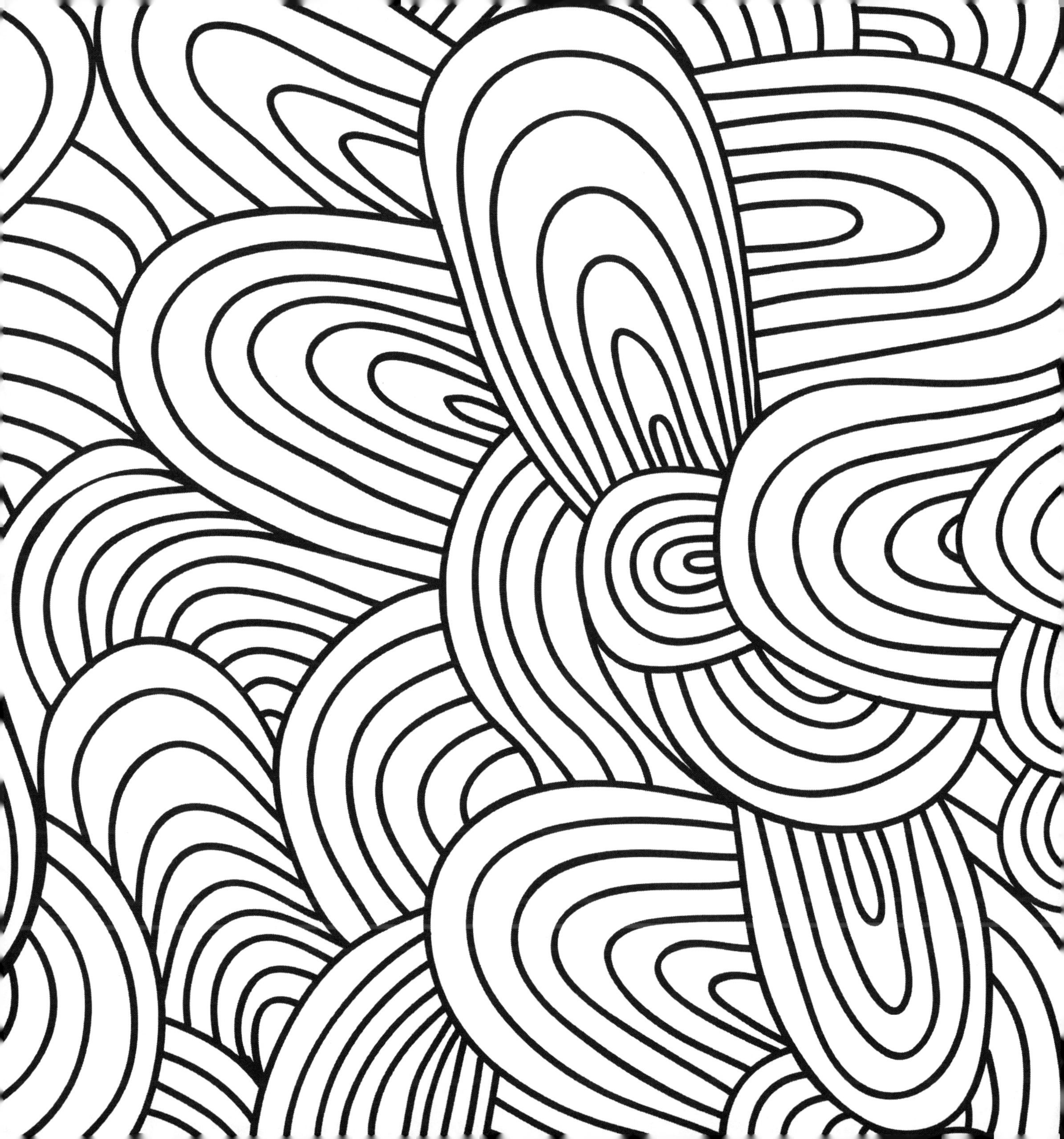

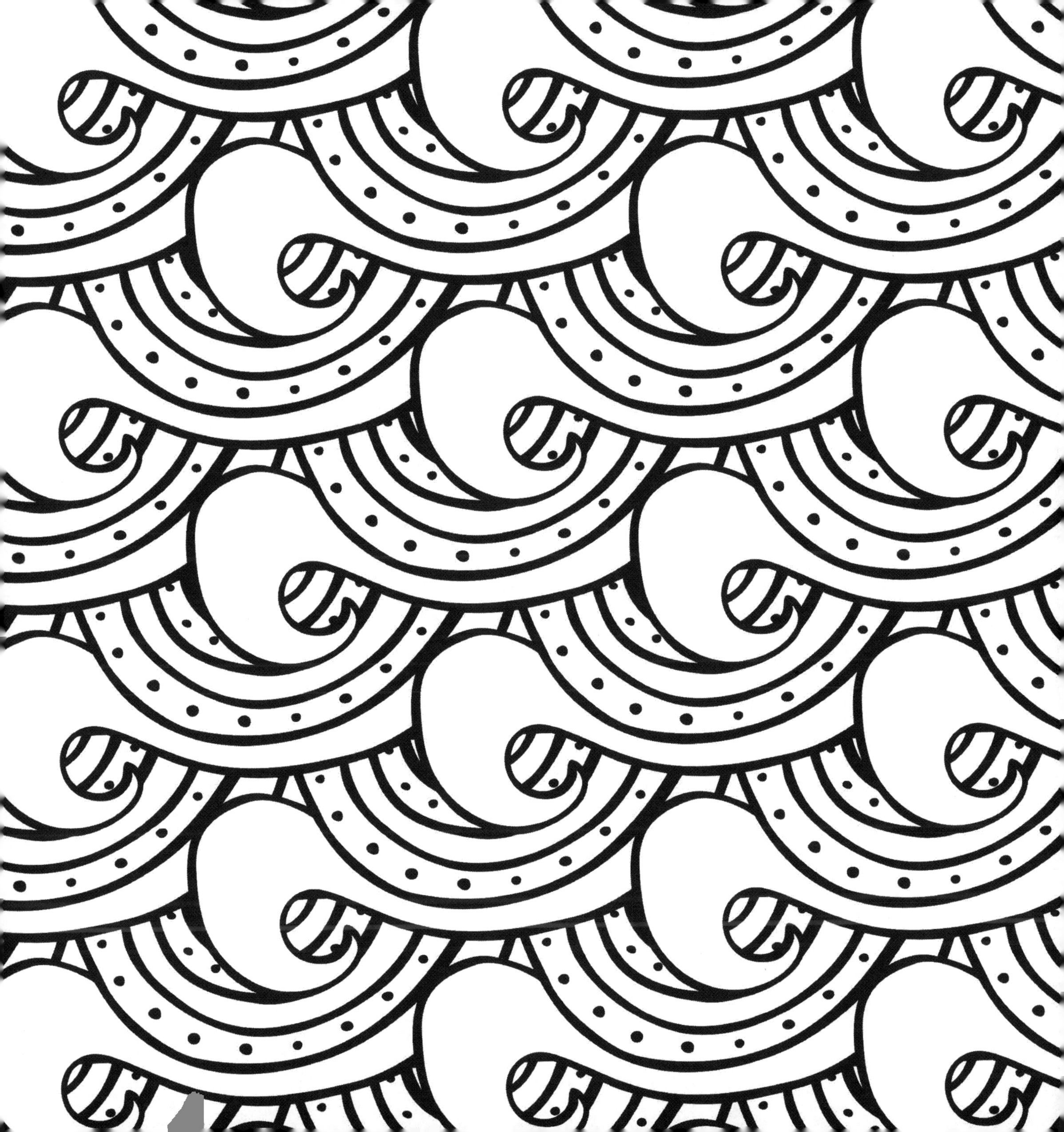

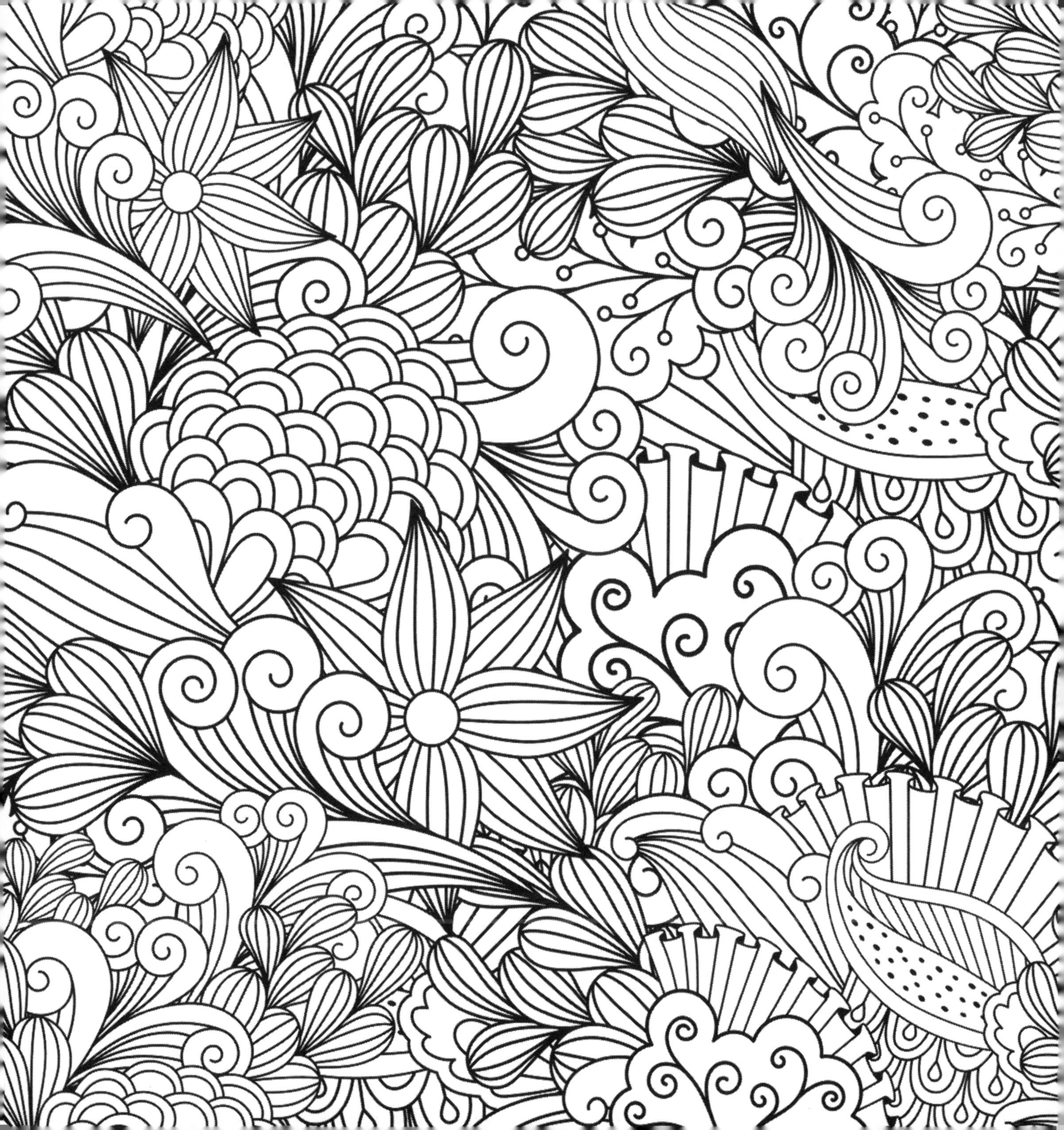

28999881R00033

Made in the USA
Columbia, SC
20 October 2018